Pandemonium

in a

Pet Shop

Ann Couchman

My True Life Adventures

Also available:

Mayhem at the Manor
Sleepless in Soho
Bedlam in a Bedsit
Ralphy to the Rescue !
Baby on a Barge
Chaos in the Computer Room
Scandals in Suburbia

This book is dedicated to the memory of
my wonderful dad
Louis Burgess

3rd November 1910 - 26th November 1984

A lovely man who kept me smiling.

Walking through the World

As I go walking through the world,
Dad, please walk with me,
And through the beauty of the world
Help me look and see.
As I go listening through the world,
Let me hear your voice,
And with the wind, the birds, the sea
Help me to rejoice.
As I go slower through this world
Give me quiet peace,
And show me, Dad, that in my life
Your love will never cease.

Introduction

My story spans the years from 1982 to 1985. The closure of my firm and the subsequent loss of my job as a computer supervisor thrust me into the daunting world of unemployment. The added responsibility of being a single parent with a son to raise and a mortgage to pay amplified the stress, taking a toll on my health.

Nevertheless, standing on the threshold of a new chapter in my life, I felt ready to embrace a career change. This would be a fresh challenge, pushing my limits.

After my divorce, I was fortunate to still have the unwavering support of my ex-in-laws, Joan and Cyril. Their encouragement was a constant source of reassurance. We had all reached a crossroads as we navigated through life's uncertainties. Their recent move from Kent to Norfolk in search of a new business venture started me thinking along the same lines.

Unfortunately, the future remains veiled from our sight. If I had the foresight to anticipate the challenges ahead, I would have made a different decision with less dire consequences. Yet, the weight of life's uncertainties and the regret for past decisions is a burden we all carry at times. But it's a burden we can overcome, fuelled by the flame of hope that lights our path and keeps us moving forward.

Pandemonium in a Pet Shop

Contents

Chapter One

In Search of a Shop

I curled up on the rug in the lounge, hugging a hot water bottle. I lay alone in my bungalow, wishing the diabolical pain in my stomach would ease up and leave me in peace.

I had met Carol in town earlier for lunch at a newly opened wine bar. Carol and I had worked at Intertruck, a company to which we had dedicated many years of our lives. I was the computer supervisor, and Carol worked in the warehouse with stock control. The firm had closed a few days earlier, leaving us unemployed and on the dole. The loss of our jobs, the uncertainty of the future, and the financial strain it brought weighed heavily on us. On our last day at work, Carol had suggested we meet in town for a meal to cheer ourselves up.

After our enjoyable lunch of chilli con carne with a glass of wine, I drove us to Carol's ground-floor flat for coffee. As we chatted, I became aware of an uncomfortable ache in my stomach that was becoming increasingly painful. I tried to ignore it, hoping it would disappear, but it didn't. I had no option but to leave and go home. I didn't mention my pain to Carol as I didn't want to worry her.

Fortunately, my eleven-year-old son, Byron, was staying with my parents, so I didn't need to worry about him. By the evening, my pain was becoming unbearable, like a knife going through me, forcing me to take shallow breaths in an attempt to minimise the pain.

Realising the pain was getting worse, not better, I finally rang the surgery and asked the doctor to call. I left the front door on the catch so the doctor could let himself in and then crawled into bed to wait.

Just before midnight, the doctor eventually arrived. After examining me, he said: "You have all the classic symptoms of an ulcer, but it can't be an ulcer because you have no history of ulcers."

I was stunned by the doctor's seemingly illogical diagnosis, but I felt too ill to argue. Despite his words, the doctor prescribed some medicine to treat an ulcer. I trusted his expertise, relieved that there was a potential solution to my agonising pain.

"Make an appointment to see me at the surgery," he said as he was leaving.

After the doctor had gone, the pain began to ease, allowing me to get some sleep. The next morning, I was left with a soreness in my stomach, so I hurried to the local chemist to collect the medicine.

A few days later, I went to the surgery for a check-up, and the doctor conceded that I did have a small ulcer after all. Recalling the agony I had suffered, I didn't consider the ulcer small. But the relief I felt, now that I knew the cause of my pain, was immense. The medicine worked well, easing any recurring pain almost instantly.

The constant worries that bugged me of losing my job, being solely responsible for raising Byron, and paying a mortgage had all taken a toll on my health, causing the ulcer. I desperately needed a break to recharge and rejuvenate.

I rang my ex-in-laws and arranged to visit them in Norfolk. Joan and Cyril are a young-at-heart couple who have been a constant source of support and comfort for me. They were there for me during my troubled marriage, offering a listening ear and practical advice. Even after my divorce from their son, Stuart, they continued to be a pillar of strength. Byron and I have cherished memories of the many holidays we enjoyed with them, camping, caravanning, and self-catering.

When Joan and Cyril moved to Norfolk a couple of years ago, they gave me their beloved caravan, a gift that holds a special place in my heart. It now stands in a parking area to one side of my driveway, its edge about one foot above the front lawn, so great care is needed when manoeuvring the caravan into position.

My younger brother, Roger, used his skills as a carpenter and builder to repair the caravan's damaged roof and make the concrete hard standing for it. In return, he uses the caravan at his race meetings with the Dartford and District Motor Club.

So far, I haven't plucked up the courage to attempt towing it. I would need a tow bar fitted to my Dolomite, but I'm in no rush to do that.

The year is 1982, and I find myself at a crucial crossroads at thirty-five years of age. I have dedicated the last nine years of my life to Intertruck, a local firm that dealt with parts for trucks. I started part-time as an invoice typist and progressed to full-time employment and promotion to computer operator and then computer supervisor.

The firm closed its doors after being bought out by a large American company who, due to the recession, decided to relocate the Dartford office to their much larger offices in Northampton. They offered me a position on their more extensive computer. However, the idea of uprooting myself and Byron from friends and family to live and work in Northampton was too unsettling. It didn't appeal to me, so I opted for redundancy.

Now, I was faced with a pivotal decision about my future. The need to find work was pressing, but the ongoing severe recession posed a significant challenge. This recession was considered the worst since the Great Depression of the 1930s. Despite the economic downturn that deepened after July 1981, I was determined to persevere.

Before leaving for Norfolk, I called in to see my parents. They lived several streets away in the Crescent, where they had lived since the houses were built after the war. My brother Roger and I grew up there, and he still lives at home.

While we were away, I arranged for him to look after Jojo, Byron's black-and-white neutered cat. He was rescued from a feral existence after being born under a wood pile at Intertruck. His litter mates shunned human contact, but Jojo was different. He decided he wanted a more leisurely, pampered life. However, if I was late with his dinner, instead of waiting, he would often disappear outside to return shortly with a mouse or a bird in his mouth, proving that he still retained his feral roots.

Jojo even tackled an enormous ferocious rat from the nearby dairy, cornering it in a pile of wood on my drive. However, when the rat opened its mouth wide, showing its long yellow fangs, and uttered a terrifying scream, Jojo wisely decided to back off and allow it to escape.

My parents were a constant source of support during my full-time work at Intertruck. They took on the responsibility of caring for Byron after school. He had attended the same infant and junior schools I once graced many years ago.

Dad, who has been retired for seven years, battles with emphasaemia, a chronic lung disease caused by years of smoking roll-ups that have damaged his lungs. His illness has reshaped their home, with his bed now occupying the dining room and an oxygen cylinder always within reach. The dining room table has been moved into the lounge to

4

make space for his bed. Having been a wartime nurse, Mum provides him with the care he needs, albeit with occasional grumbles about the extra work.

I admit I have always been the apple of my dad's eye, whereas Mum has made it quite clear that Roger is her favourite. In my younger years, I vowed that if I ever had more than one child, I would definitely not show favouritism as it could lead to much anguish. Fortunately, I didn't have to deal with this problem because I only had Byron.

Byron and I drove to Swanton Morley, a mid-Norfolk village, for a holiday with Joan and Cyril at the end of July. They had moved to Norfolk at the end of September 1980, intent on buying a business, but so far hadn't found the right one. They were searching for a shop with accommodation included. In the meantime, they were living at their daughter Stella's house, as it was more convenient for them to stay there while hunting for the right property.

Stella and her husband, Mick, spent most of their time in Saudi Arabia, working in large warehouses stocktaking hospital equipment. The pay was excellent and enabled them to afford the mortgage on their house in Norfolk.

I drew up on the drive of the modern three-bedroom semi. I parked behind Cyril's new Lada estate, which he had bought ready to do cash and carry once they had bought a shop.

Joan rushed out to greet us, giving us both a big hug. She absolutely doted on her grandson. Joan was a slim, attractive, energetic woman. "It's lovely to see you both again," she said, helping me carry our cases indoors.

Over dinner, I told my in-laws about the events leading up to Intertruck's closure and my recent health issue. Joan and Cyril listened intently, their concern evident.

"Cyril is a born worrier, so I'm surprised he doesn't suffer from ulcers," Joan said.

5

Cyril gave a wry smile. "That minor heart attack I had was a wake-up call, a stark reminder for me to take things easier."

His health scare, seven years ago in 1975, when he ended up in hospital, had been of grave concern. It had also been the catalyst for him to give up smoking, a commitment he has upheld ever since.

"It was a big worry at the time, but at least it gave you sufficient incentive to stop smoking," Joan declared.

Cyril had quite a distinguished look with his dark hair, sideburns and Mexican moustache. Yet he tended to be a little self-conscious of his prominent nose.

"I shall feel relieved once we find the right shop to run," he said. "So far, we haven't found a business with a good enough turnover. There was the deli at Holt, a quaint, bustling Georgian town. I really liked that shop nestled in a quiet courtyard, but we were too slow putting in an offer, so we missed out on that little gold mine."

Joan, always the optimist, smiled. "Don't worry, Cyril, we'll find something else just as good," she assured him.

After they both became unemployed, they made the bold decision to sell their executive Georgian-style house near Maidstone to fund the purchase of a shop. Cyril was convinced that, at his age, in his mid-fifties, he was now too old for any employer to hire him.

I worried Joan and Cyril might fritter away their life savings before they found a shop, knowing how carefree they were with money. They had already treated themselves to extravagant holidays in America and Saudi Arabia.

"Tomorrow, we'll celebrate your wedding anniversary," I announced excitedly. "Byron and I can't wait to treat you to a special meal."

"Oh, that would be wonderful!" Joan exclaimed.

"Do you know a good restaurant where you would like to have a meal?" I asked.

"There's a charming French restaurant just outside Norwich that we've fancied trying but haven't had the chance yet," Cyril said. He enjoyed cooking and thought of himself as a bit of a gourmet. The kitchen had always been his domain, as Joan freely admitted being hopeless at cooking.

"Then that's where we'll go," I declared. "I'll book a table."

The following evening, the meal was a resounding success. As the wine flowed, Joan was moved to tears when Byron, in a moment of unexpected thoughtfulness, stood up and toasted his grandparents.

"Here's to Grandma and Grandad – the best grandparents in the world. Happy anniversary." His heartfelt words took us all by surprise. I felt proud of my son's grown-up, impromptu action.

Joan and Cyril had snails as a starter, while Byron and I tried frog legs. We found the texture and taste similar to chicken wings. For the delicious main course, we chose lamb cooked in a wine sauce and a delectable fruit torte for dessert.

The next day, the weather remained warm, so I relaxed in the garden, sunbathing. Byron was indoors, engrossed in the new Atari computer game that Stella had recently bought. He and Joan each had a control paddle and were engaged in a lively competitive game of Breakout. Stella had acquired most of the popular games, including Pacman, Pele's Soccer, Asteroids and the newly released Defender. I could hear their yells of delight coming through the open patio doors from the lounge.

Over breakfast the following morning, Joan suggested visiting Felbrigg Hall near Cromer. Since joining the National Trust after moving to Stella's house, Joan and Cyril enjoyed exploring the many stately homes in Norfolk.

We drove to north Norfolk and parked in the car park at Felbrigg. We were immediately struck by the breathtaking grandeur of the 17th-century English country mansion. The Jacobean style architecture, built for William and Thomas Wyndham, exuded a sense of history and splendour that was truly awe-inspiring. These days, the property is under the careful preservation of the National Trust.

Inside, we were impressed by the opulent English Renaissance rooms and the charm of the Georgian and Victorian chambers, with their sumptuous four-poster beds offering a fascinating glimpse of bygone eras.

The sprawling grounds had winding paths marked out for walks in Felbrigg Woods, which were part of the estate. Byron, always full of energy, enjoyed playing a spirited game of hide and seek behind the trees with his equally lively grandma.

Cyril and I strolled along, listening to the occasional 'warble, warble' coming from Joan or Byron as they called out to each other. Cyril asked me if I had found suitable work yet, which reminded me of the uncertainties of my current situation.

I shook my head. "I've scoured the classifieds but didn't see anything that appealed to me."

"Why not consider buying a shop like we hope to do?" Cyril suggested. "Leasehold shops aren't that expensive. You've got your redundancy payment, which you could use. It could be a promising venture for you."

"Yes, that's true, but I haven't given any thought to owning a shop. I've no idea what sort of shop I'd be interested in running."

"You'll need to check the profit margins – ensure the goods you sell make a healthy profit. And don't forget about the leasehold costs and other expenses. It's a big decision, so it's important to be cautious and consider all aspects. Nevertheless, it could be a viable option for you," Cyril advised.

His words gave me food for thought. "Well, if I don't find any office or computer work, then it might be another avenue to explore."

Byron and I came down to the kitchen the next morning, where we found Joan and Cyril preparing breakfast. Their voices blended in perfect harmony as they sang 'Beautiful Brown Eyes'.

"You sound so good together," I remarked. "You should harmonise more often." I was often struck by their closeness, having grown up together. They had known each other since their school days, and I suspected they were probably soul mates.

"How do you and Byron fancy going to the Thursford Steam Museum today?" Joan suggested over breakfast. "I know Byron would love to see the musical organs, and they even have an Edwardian fairground ride." She turned to Byron. "You'd enjoy a ride on a fairground horse, wouldn't you?"

He grinned. "'Course I would, Grandma."

Cyril drove us to Thursford, a small village renowned for its steam museum, created by George Cushing. Now an elderly man, he still enjoyed working with his collection of steam engines and organs, each with its own unique sound and history. He could always be found strolling around the museum, chatting with people, sharing stories and memories.

As we walked from the car park to the entrance, a miniature steam train chugged past, offering rides around the perimeter of the grounds.

We marvelled at the array of steam engines inside the vast barn. Then we joined a group following a man who went from one fairground organ to the next, bringing them to life with lively music bursting forth and animated figures playing instruments or conducting. We watched, fascinated by the various displays; then Byron's eyes lit up when he spotted the fairground ride.

9

We all climbed aboard, Joan and Cyril choosing a lavishly upholstered open carriage, while Byron and I opted for the hard saddles of the horses. We clung onto a horse each while Joan and Cyril relaxed in the comfort of a carriage. The ride was a whirlwind of excitement, leaving us all feeling exhilarated and giddy.

It was time for everyone to take their seats for the main event. We went over to an area where seats were set out in rows, facing a magnificent Wurlitzer organ that took centre stage. The grand range of massive organ pipes was housed at the back of the stage, providing powerful sound.

The organist, Robert Wolfe, was resident there every summer. His playing left his audience utterly spellbound. Screens suspended from the rafters hung above the stage, showing close-ups of his hands and feet moving at high speed as he replicated the sound of a train roaring along or accompanied the film clips of old silent movies. He was also happy to play requests handed to him before the performance.

At the end of the enjoyable show, we headed for home. On the way, I spotted a signpost for Grimston. "One of my oldest friends lives in that village," I said. "I was Katy Bullinaire's bridesmaid back in 1964, and Dad gave her away at her wedding to Keith."

"Then you must call in and see her," Joan insisted. "Cyril, take that turning."

He quickly braked and made a sharp turn.

"Oh, but I don't know her address," I said.

"We'll make some enquiries," Joan declared. "Somebody is bound to know in a village."

Katy and I grew up together as neighbours in the Crescent. After their marriage, Katy and Keith moved to Norfolk, and we lost touch. The prospect of seeing her again after all these years filled me with excitement.

We arrived at a junction in the village where a long main road ran through it. We stopped outside a Post Office store.

"I'm sure they will know the address," Joan said confidently.

Joan and I entered the shop, and I gave the postmistress Katy's name.

She thought for a moment, then shook her head. "The name sounds familiar, but I don't know the address." Just then, the postman came in to collect the mail. "Ah, here's a man who might be able to help you."

With a glimmer of hope, I asked him if he knew Katy's address. His face lit up straight away. "You just follow me – I'm going in that direction," he said.

I thanked him, and we went outside to tell Cyril: "Follow that post van." The van led us down a couple of side roads and stopped at the end of a cul-de-sac. The postman pointed to a chalet bungalow directly in front of us, then he beeped his horn and drove away.

Cyril waited in the car with Byron while Joan and I knocked on the front door. Katy came to the door and gasped in surprise.

"Ann!" she exclaimed. "What a wonderful surprise. It's been so long." We hugged, and I introduced Joan. Cyril got out of the car and brought Byron over, so I introduced them, too.

Katy and Keith had two boys older than Byron. So many years had passed that we had not met each other's children until now. Katy was on her own as Keith was at work and her two boys were out.

She welcomed us into her home, and we spent a delightful time catching up on the events of the past eighteen years. The joy of reconnecting with Katy, of reminiscing about our past and present lives, filled me with a warm sense of nostalgia. As we said goodbye, we promised to keep in touch, cherishing our renewed bond of friendship.

On the last day of our holiday, I relaxed on the lawn, basking in the warm sunshine as the weather remained hot. Meanwhile, Byron amused himself by playing the exciting

Atari games, once again challenging his grandma to a friendly match.

Over dinner, Joan and Cyril told me about the various shops they had viewed.

"If we find the right one, it could set us up to be comfortably off in our retirement," Cyril said.

"People don't normally like to sell if the business is doing really well," Joan pointed out. "So we have to look for the unexplored potential in the business."

"Although it sounds quite challenging," I said, "perhaps I should consider running a shop as you suggested, Cyril; after all, I have my redundancy pay. I could use it to buy a lease on a shop."

"A bank would be happy to lend you the money to set up a business because you've got your bungalow to use as collateral," Joan pointed out.

"The more I think about owning a shop, the more it appeals to me," I declared.

"Well, we think it's a good idea," Cyril said. "You keep your independence since you're the boss." He had always valued his independence.

"I think I'll check out what shops are currently on the market when I get home."

"What type of shop would you like to run?" Joan asked.

I thought for a moment. "I suppose my ideal shop would be a pet shop. I adore the atmosphere of pet shops. All the different aromas of the feeds, the scent of hay and straw, are wonderful. And, of course, the animals for sale – I'm always tempted to buy one. I could never walk past the pet shop in Dartford without stopping to gaze in the window and admire the monkey in its cage in the covered entrance." My memories of that pet shop came flooding back.

"If you recall, friends of ours owned that pet shop," Joan said. "I asked them to order you and Stuart a pair of white fan-tailed doves when you lived on the barge."

I smiled. "Yes, when we were first married, we had romantic ideas. I think you came up with the idea of us keeping doves. They were beautiful, and watching them circling over the Medway River was thrilling."

"That monkey of theirs was a vicious thing," Cyril said. "There was a warning on its cage not to put your fingers inside, or they would get bitten."

"It was an adorable little monkey, though. However, thinking about what type of shop I might like; alternatively, I wouldn't mind a corner shop or perhaps a wool shop," I added.

"Do check the accounts very carefully to ensure the business is profitable," Cyril advised, returning to the practicalities of owning a shop.

Then, we reminisced about our past holidays, the shared experiences and the laughter that made those times so special.

The next day, after an early lunch, Byron and I reluctantly left to return home. We hugged Joan and Cyril and thanked them for a lovely holiday.

Little did I realise the journey ahead would be far from the leisurely drive I had anticipated. "We'll be home long before it gets dark," I declared confidently, settling into the driver's seat. Ever since the problem I had with my headlights dimming, I didn't trust driving the Dolomite at night.

But I was wrong. I had only been driving for twenty minutes when the sky became overcast, and the rain came down in torrents. The sky quickly turned pitch dark like night as the weather deteriorated into a bad summer storm with deafening thunderclaps and lightning forking overhead. I had to use my headlights as I struggled to see the road. The rain pounded on the roof and windscreen. Even the wipers, moving at full speed, couldn't clear the windscreen sufficiently for me to see where I was going. I was gripped with fear and uncertainty, desperately wanting to pull over and stop, but there was nowhere to do this. All

I could do was follow the car in front, my only beacon of hope in the darkness.

'So much for not wanting to drive home in the dark,' I thought grimly as I tried to determine where I was heading. I had never known a storm so bad that it turned day into the blackest night. The thunder continued to crash, and it wasn't until I reached the M11 that the storm eased up and the darkness lifted. To finally see the road ahead was a welcome relief.

Back home, my mind was buzzing with Joan and Cyril's words about the potential of buying a shop. The idea intrigued me, so I bought a local paper, eager to explore the classifieds. I came across an agency that had several shops for sale. I called them and requested some details to be sent to me.

When the package arrived in the post, one set of particulars caught my attention. They were for a wool and baby-wear shop in a nearby town. The idea of running this type of business interested me. I called the agent and scheduled an appointment to view the shop on Sunday when it would be closed.

As Byron was now a sensible eleven-year-old, I felt I could safely leave him at home while visiting the shop.

I parked my car outside a small parade of shops. My attention was immediately drawn to the neat, modern shop with a flat above it. As I stepped inside, a middle-aged lady emerged from the back room, her warm smile and friendly handshake making me feel instantly welcome.

She showed me her well-stocked shelves behind a long counter containing a wide variety of wools. On the other side of the shop, baby clothes, along with some toys and accessories, were displayed.

"I source all my wool and baby clothes from a reputable warehouse in the East End of London," the lady informed me. "I usually make a trip there once a month, loading up my van with new stock." Then she opened the till to show me the till roll, which detailed the takings for the previous day.

"Saturdays are always the busiest days, as you can see if you compare yesterday's takings to earlier days in the week." She unravelled the roll to show me the figures. The potential for a thriving business was evident. I could visualise myself working there quite happily. The shop was clean and tidy, and all the goods were tastefully displayed.

The lady took me upstairs to show me around the flat. It boasted two double bedrooms, a spacious lounge with picture windows overlooking the street and a fitted kitchen with ample space for a table. The well-maintained flat presented a promising opportunity for additional income through rental.

I left feeling quite excited at the prospect of running a wool shop. However, a niggling doubt about the practicality of cash and carry at an East End warehouse slightly dampened my spirits.

I decided to keep an open mind and view some more shops before reaching any decision. The next shop I viewed was a lock-up-and-leave dress shop at Erith.

As I walked in, the shop struck me as old-fashioned and dowdy. Some of the dresses looked decidedly frumpy. The elderly lady who greeted me explained about the top brand names she stocked. "They are what my customers like to wear," she said, removing a dress from a rack to show me the label. I got the impression the dresses were also what this lady liked to wear.

"I employ a part-time seamstress who does any necessary alterations," the lady informed me, returning the dress to the rack and leading me to a small, cluttered back room where another elderly lady sat at a sewing machine amongst a jumble of clothes, busily making changes to a dress.

"This is Geraldine," the lady said, introducing me to her seamstress. "She would be happy to continue working for whoever takes over the shop. I intend to retire, but I would be willing to give any advice or help that might be needed."

I drove home, wondering if there was any future in such an old-fashioned shop. It was crying out for a fresh, modern touch, a revamp with the latest fashions. A complete overhaul of the shop's inventory would be needed, which would be a significant undertaking, making me question the practicality of this business. With no experience in the fashion industry, I felt it was a challenge beyond my reach, so I dismissed this shop out of hand. However, viewing these shops was a valuable learning experience.

I rang Joan that evening to tell her about the two shops I had viewed.

"I'm glad you're taking your time and not rushing into anything," Joan told me. "I can't imagine you running an old-fashioned dress shop. The wool shop sounds like a possibility, but I'm sure you'll find something more appealing."

Joan had some news for me. "Stuart is now living in Norfolk. They moved into a modern house at Fakenham a couple of weeks ago, and he's started work at a nearby private hospital. He seems to be enjoying the change and the new opportunities."

Stuart was now married to Murni, a Malaysian nurse, and they had two children, a baby boy and a little girl. He mentioned a job offer at a private mental hospital in Norfolk earlier in the year. I was happy for Stuart's new venture but also concerned about the potential impact on Byron, as this meant he would see far less of his dad.

"You'll be able to see your other grandchildren more often now they aren't too far away," I said, trying to sound upbeat. Byron had been the sole grandchild for many years. However, he now had to get accustomed to sharing his grandma and grandad – something he seemed to accept with no difficulty, unlike me.

I had always resented Murni, probably unfairly, for breaking up my marriage. Back then, it had been just as much Stuart's fault. But now that Stuart and I have moved on with our lives, I realise the time has come to let go of this resentment. I hung up the phone, resolving to do just that.

When I received intriguing details about a delicatessen in the outlying village of Hartley, it immediately reminded me of Cyril's enthusiasm for the deli at Holt, boasting impressive profit margins. I felt optimistic about exploring this potential investment, seeing it as a promising project.

Arriving at the shop the following Saturday, I found it tucked in the corner of a small square of modern shops. Joining a queue of customers, I observed the man behind the counter weighing the various cooked meats and cheeses, each transaction accompanied by a cheerful word.

This pleasant atmosphere brought back memories of my brief stint working part-time at a deli counter in a small local supermarket when I was first married, so I was familiar with the work.

Once the customers had been served, the man turned his attention to me. He took me through to a backroom and showed me where the food was stored in a large cold room. He explained what sort of turnover the shop made each week and, as I expected, told me about the excellent profit margins.

As I drove home, I mulled over the man's words. The shop seemed like a sound investment, but it was hard to muster enthusiasm for running a deli and serving meat, cheese, and pies all day. My memories of the few hours I spent each day in the deli all those years ago didn't fill me with a burning desire to return to that line of work.

More details of another shop for sale arrived through my letterbox. This time, it was a curtain shop on the outskirts of London. With nothing better to do, I made an appointment to view the shop, though I didn't have high hopes of it being the sort of shop that would appeal to me.

I found the bright, airy lock-up shop in the middle of a small parade of modern, similar-sized shops. The neat, middle-aged lady owner showed me the wide range of curtains and blinds she sold.

"I have a small army of machinists who work from home making bespoke curtains," the lady explained with a sense of pride. "I go to the customers' homes to take the measurements, and they select the material from the variety of swatches I have. As you can see, I also keep a selection of ready-made curtains here for display and an assortment of blinds."

I couldn't help but be impressed with the lady's work. However, I felt the whole business depended on the reliability of the women employed to work from home. I didn't feel sufficiently confident to take on such a responsibility.

As I suspected, this type of business didn't appeal to me. It was disappointing to once again dismiss the shop as unsuitable. I was beginning to understand why Joan and Cyril had such difficulty finding the right business.

December arrived, and with Christmas approaching, I needed a break from searching for a shop. I decided to treat Mum and myself to a special evening at the Royal Albert Hall, watching a performance of the Hallelujah Chorus. Byron stayed with his grandad as neither of them was a fan of such events. Besides, Dad would have found the journey far too tiring in his incapacitated condition.

We caught the train to London and then the tube, which brought us almost to the Royal Albert Hall. The grandeur of the Hall, with its majestic architecture, was a sight to behold. We stopped to buy sweets in the foyer and then made our way upstairs to find our seats.

We were mesmerised as we listened to the enthralling music from Handel's Messiah. The superb acoustics in the Hall enhanced the singing. It was renowned for highlighting the slightest noise, as I discovered to my consternation when I attempted to unwrap a sweet. The rustling wrapper echoed around the dome, causing some disapproving glances in my direction. I had to wait for the interval before I could finish unwrapping the sweet.

Byron and I spent a quiet, cosy Christmas at home. We enjoyed a brief visit to my parents on Boxing Day. After returning home, I rang Joan and Cyril to wish them a happy Christmas. Stella and Mick were home from Saudi Arabia over the festive season.

"Stella and Mick are trying for a baby," Joan said excitedly. "I guessed Stella wouldn't want to wait too long before starting a family once they were married."

"I suppose she'll be coming home to live once there's a baby on the way," I said.

"Yes, but by then, we'll have moved out and started running a business," Joan said. "I think Mick intends to continue working in Saudi as it's the only way they can afford the mortgage."

"It doesn't sound ideal for a married couple to be living so far apart," I surmised, feeling concerned. I recalled Stella's failed relationship with her long-time boyfriend, Pete when they shared a house. He spent so much time at work that she became bored and ran off with Mick.

"You're right," Joan agreed. "I can't imagine Stella wanting a long-distance marriage for too long. It's a tough situation for them, but I'm sure they'll work it out. Perhaps Mick will consider finding work back in this country."

The dawn of 1983 was filled with anticipation and excitement, heralding significant change with the introduction of breakfast television. On January 17th, a new era began as Frank Bough, the host of the BBC morning show, graced our screens in a refreshing departure from the newsreaders in their formal suits.

In his relaxed style, wearing a jumper, Frank introduced the viewers to the Green Goddess for a daily workout, marking the beginning of a fresh television experience.

TV AM swiftly copied this, broadcasting Good Morning Britain in direct competition with the BBC.

As February unfolded, the stark reality of the times hit home. Unemployment figures soared to a record high of well over three million. I found myself among these millions, grappling with the harsh reality of unemployment.

The first day of March saw the advent of the CD, a new technology offering improved quality to music. This was a significant moment in the history of music, as CDs were now for sale in record shops across the UK for the first time, marking a monumental shift from the era of vinyl records to the digital age of music.

Meanwhile, I received details of a corner shop for sale only a few streets away. Being so close to home, it was worth viewing. The idea of owning a general store, where I could buy my weekly groceries at cost price, was undeniably appealing and could be helpful. I had walked past this shop many times and knew it well.

A few days later, I arrived at closing time to be shown around by the lady owner. The compact shop was impressively well-stocked with essential groceries, plus a freezer and chilled cabinet offering various products. She showed me the stock room at the rear and also the small two-bedroom flat upstairs.

However, the prospect of working such long hours, seven days a week, to make the shop pay left me feeling disillusioned. I didn't want to become another Arkwright like the character from the comedy television series, 'Open All Hours.' The thought of being stuck in this small shop week in, week out made me realise I would soon become bored, and so, once again, it became a non-starter.

I received a phone call from my friend, Dave. He was the manager of the bus garage at Swanley. His divorce from his wife, Penny, now they had split up, had yet to be finalised by his solicitor. They had a daughter, Natasha, who was a couple of years younger than Byron.

Dave was once Stuart's best friend, having grown up together. He regarded Joan and Cyril as surrogate parents after losing his own at a young age. Dave had reached a point where he could no longer tolerate Penny's numerous affairs. Having suffered Stuart's infidelities when we were married, I could sympathise with Dave at this challenging time.

"I've been busy redecorating the house, and now I want to furnish it in a style of *my* choosing. Would you come with me into town and help me choose some new furniture?"

I agreed, pleased to be a part of this new chapter in Dave's life. He arranged to collect me the following day. Byron and I had enjoyed many holidays with Dave, Penny, Natasha, Joan, and Cyril over the years. Dave's quick-witted humour made him good company. He and Cyril sparked off each other, trying to outdo the other with their witty repartees.

Dave arrived the next day, and we drove into town in his Mini. We headed for the large department store that specialised in a wide range of furniture and spent some time trying out the various armchairs and settees. Then, a salesman approached us, keen to offer his expertise.

"I'm looking for something in leather," Dave informed him. The salesman's face lit up with enthusiasm as he led us across the expansive room to a group of leather armchairs.

"Perhaps your wife would like to try one of these?" he suggested. Dave and I exchanged a knowing glance, and I giggled, unable to contain my amusement. I sat in a red chair, and Dave sat in one next to me.

The salesman, oblivious to his blunder, continued with his sales pitch. "These are club chairs in ox-blood red," he informed us. "It's a traditional style and colour."

Dave stood up and beamed at the salesman. "My wife and I will take these two chairs and a matching sofa," he declared, giving me a wink when the salesman wasn't looking.

After Dave had made arrangements for the delivery of the furniture, we went into a cafe in the nearby arcade for a celebratory coffee. Dave stirred his coffee, looking thoughtful, and then smiled at me. "I liked what the salesman said, mistaking you for my wife. It sounded good."

"You really ought to have corrected him," I chided.

"He had no right to make such an assumption," Dave said, his tone indignant but his eyes twinkling with mischief. "But I didn't mind – did you?"

I smiled. "No, of course not. I found it quite amusing."

We finished our coffee, and then Dave drove me home.

On the way, Dave casually mentioned that he also needed furniture for his dining room. "I fancy getting a mahogany table and chairs in a classic Regency style with striped material on the seats," he said.

"I've seen some reproduction Regency furniture in my catalogue," I said. "Come in when we get home, and I'll show you."

Indoors, I dug out my catalogue from a cupboard in the lounge and flicked through it to the section showing dining room furniture.

"That's exactly what I had in mind!" Dave exclaimed.

"I'll be happy to order it for you. And as my valued customer, you can comfortably spread the payments over several months," I said, eager to help.

"That sounds perfect. I'll go for an extendable table and six chairs, two of them with arms. Finally, my house will reflect *my* taste," Dave declared with a hint of excitement.

He left with a spring in his step. "You must come over and see the place once it's all kitted out," he yelled as he climbed into his Mini and waved goodbye.

Easter arrived on April 3rd, and Stella and Mick had come home for a brief break. Joan rang one evening to ask how the search for a shop was progressing.

I sighed. "Not very well. I'm having the same problems as you. Finding the right business is tricky and also frustrating."

"You'll know when the right shop comes along," Joan assured me. She was always optimistic and encouraged me not to give up. "We're still looking for a lucrative shop, but in the meantime, I'm thinking about returning to office work, probably in Norwich. I feel the need to be doing something. Stella and Mick send their love. So far, they haven't had any luck starting a family, but they have plenty of time."

After wishing them well, I hung up, wondering if I, too, should consider returning to office work. I felt in need of a break from searching for a shop. None of the ones I had viewed had really resonated with me. I hoped Joan was right, and the perfect shop would eventually come my way, saying: "Buy me – you'll love working here!"

Chapter Two

Tia Maria

Since my childhood, I have always yearned to own a pedigree cat. Several years ago, I finally realised my dream when I bought a beautiful Siamese kitten called Cassie. But a few months later, I was devastated to lose her.

Now, I felt the time had come to replace her. I loved the Siamese's markings and vivid blue eyes, so I searched the classifieds in the local paper. However, what caught my attention wasn't a Siamese kitten but a Colourpoint Persian. These had the same markings and blue eyes as the Siamese but with the cobby body, neat ears and luxurious fur of a Persian.

A litter was advertised with an Erith phone number. I quickly called and arranged to go and see these kittens. I had my heart set on a seal point female, with the intention of breeding in the future.

When I arrived at the lady's house, an attractive, slim brunette about my age introduced herself as Debbie. She showed me into her lounge, where four adorable kittens were frolicking in a pen.

"I'm afraid there's only one kitten still available," she informed me. I could see a seal point and hoped this was the one left.

Debbie carefully lifted a kitten from the pen and placed her in my arms. She wasn't the seal point I had initially hoped for, but as I looked down at the beautiful little face staring inquisitively at me, suddenly, it didn't matter. A sense of joy filled my heart. This kitten was special in her own unique way, and I felt an instant connection with her, a bond that would only grow stronger with time.

"This is a blue-cream little girl," Debbie said. "My friend is having the seal point girl, and I'm keeping the blue point girl. The red point boy is going to an elderly couple as a pet. I am so pleased with this litter. All three girls are suitable for breeding and also have show qualities. The boy is the only pet-quality kitten."

I was thrilled to hear this. "I was hoping to breed from her one day," I told Debbie.

"Well, the mother cat is also a blue-cream. I mated her to a seal point boy, and as you can see, there is the possibility of a wider range of colours with a blue-cream breeding queen, depending on the colour of the stud cat you use. I would have kept her myself, but since I already have a blue-cream, I chose the blue point girl instead. They have a good pedigree – I'll show it to you."

Debbie went over to a dresser and opened a drawer. She handed me a certificate showing five generations of cats with several champions, including the grandsire of these kittens.

"This kitten has the registered name of Tia Maria."

"Oh, that is such a pretty name!" I exclaimed. Just then, the phone rang, and Debbie went to answer it.

She spoke into the phone and then turned to me. "Have you decided to take Tia? Only I've got someone on the phone who wants to come and see her."

"Oh, yes, please," I said straight away, hugging the kitten. I didn't want to ever let her go.

Debbie hung up the phone and went through the paperwork with me.

"How would you feel about showing your kitten?" she asked.

I was taken aback. "I've never considered entering her in a cat show," I admitted.

"Well, she's definitely good enough. My friend and I intend to enter our kittens in the Kensington, Kitten and Neuter show in August. Why not enter Tia, too?"

"But, I've no idea how to enter her for a show."

Debbie smiled. "Oh, don't worry. I'll guide you through the process," she assured me.

"That would be marvellous!" I felt so relieved. "I'm really looking forward to my first cat show."

I carefully put Tia in the cat basket I had brought, and Debbie gave me some kitten food to take home.

"There is just one check I need to make," Debbie said as I was leaving. "I'll come to your house next week to vet your property and ensure that Tia is happy in her new home. I always do this whenever a kitten goes to a new home."

I left feeling a little worried. 'What if Debbie thinks my home is unsuitable and takes Tia away?' The thought of losing her was unbearable. She had already stolen my heart and was now an irreplaceable part of my life.

I was bursting with pride as I brought my beautiful Tia to my parents' house to show her off. Her charm was irresistible, and she instantly won over my parents, especially Dad, who was eager for his sister to meet Tia.

"I can imagine your Auntie Rene's delight when she sees Tia. Let's pop round there now," he suggested.

My Auntie Rene and Uncle Harold lived just a few streets away, so we were soon knocking on their door. Tia basked in all the fuss and attention she received. My aunt was so pleased that I had brought Tia for her to see.

I told her about the surprising amount of grooming necessary to keep Tia's coat in top condition. She was amazed at the dedication and care involved, using baby talc to keep the coat fluffy.

Two days later, Mum and Dad called in at my bungalow. They presented me with a gift for Tia from Auntie Rene, namely some baby talcum powder. I was touched by my aunt's thoughtful gesture.

Byron had been repairing his bicycle in the unfinished dining room extension that my brother had recently built. Since being made redundant, the work had come to a halt. It was still awaiting the second fix of electrics and a coat of paint, but in the meantime, it made a useful room where Byron could work on his bike.

Tia's litter tray was also kept in this room. She had settled in well and made friends with Jojo. I nervously cleaned and tidied up, preparing for Debbie's visit. I made sure Tia was meticulously groomed and spruced up, ready to meet her breeder. I felt a twinge of resentment at Debbie's intrusion into my home to check its suitability. However, I understood she was only doing it with the best of intentions for Tia's happiness.

When Debbie arrived, I ushered her into the kitchen and put the kettle on for tea. Debbie was keen to see Tia. She spotted her in the dining room and called her. Tia came bounding into the kitchen, pleased to see her breeder again.

I was mortified to see a large smudge of black oil on Tia's back. She had rubbed under Byron's bike. I apologised to Debbie, worried that she would think me an irresponsible pet owner, allowing my new kitten to get covered in oil.

Debbie just laughed it off. "Kittens get into all sorts of mischief," she said, taking the mug of tea I handed her. "I can see she has a good, loving home here and seems perfectly happy."

I breathed a sigh of relief, realising I had successfully passed Debbie's home check. "You will let me have the necessary entry papers for the cat show you mentioned, won't you?" I asked, my confidence restored.

"Yes, of course, I will. Why don't you bring Tia over to my house one day? Then I can demonstrate how to prepare her coat for the show."

"That's very kind of you," I said, grateful for all her help. I was a complete novice when it came to showing a pedigree kitten, so I was eager to learn from Debbie's expertise.

A few weeks later, I rang Debbie and arranged to take Tia to her house, as we had agreed.

I arrived with Tia in her wicker basket one Saturday morning. Debbie greeted us at the door with a warm smile. Her husband was out at work, so we had the house to ourselves.

"I should warn you that Tia will hiss at me when you let her out of the basket," Debbie said as I put the basket on the lounge carpet.

"Oh, surely not!" I was taken aback by the unexpected warning. "Tia is such a friendly kitten."

Debbie laughed. "It's just something all kittens do if they return to their breeder's home - I don't know why."

I released Tia from the basket, and, right on cue, she hissed at Debbie. Debbie gave her a cuddle, and Tia soon purred contentedly, all resentment forgotten. Tia was pleased to see her litter mate, the blue point kitten Debbie had named Tiffany. Both kittens had grown quite a lot over the past few weeks.

We took Tia to the bathroom, where Debbie washed Tia's fur with baby shampoo. "You must be careful not to get soapy water in her eyes or ears," she explained. Then she rinsed her coat using the shower head, rubbed Tia with a towel, and put her back in the cat basket.

"Now, she needs to be dried using a hair dryer," Debbie said as we returned downstairs. Tia didn't object to the washing, though she was less keen on having her coat blown about by the hair dryer. She squirmed in the basket, clearly not enjoying the confinement or the noise of the hair dryer.

Once Tia was dry, Debbie demonstrated the grooming routine for the show. She sprinkled baby talc on Tia's coat, rubbed it in, and then brushed her coat thoroughly. "You'll need to bath her a week before the show, and then talc and brush her coat twice a day until the day of the show," she advised. "On the show day, focus on brushing her coat to remove all the excess talc. This is crucial for the vetting-in stage at the cat show. Remember to finish by brushing the coat the wrong way to fluff it up and always brush her trousers away from her rear."

Using a cotton bud, Debbie checked her ears to ensure they were clean and wiped around her eyes with moistened cotton wool.

"This is a little ruse I learnt to make the ears look neater," she said, holding the tip of each ear firmly between her finger and thumb and plucking any hairs sticking up. "A Persian cat's ears should be small, neat, rounded and well spread apart. That's what the judges look for." She finished off by carefully brushing around Tia's face, using a clean toothbrush to fluff up the fur."

I sighed. "There's so much to learn about preparing a kitten for a show."

"Oh, you'll soon get the hang of it," Debbie assured me. "Besides, I'll be with you at your first show to ensure you do everything right. Here's an entry form for you to complete and send off," she added, handing me a form. "The show isn't until August, but the form must be sent in by the closing date. Having all three of my girl kittens competing at the show will be so exciting!"

One evening during the week, I received a phone call from Dave.

"I'm taking a bus to the air show at Lakenheath on Saturday. Do you and Byron fancy a day out? I've got Natasha for the weekend, so she'll be coming, too. It's going to be a fantastic day!"

29

"That sounds great!" I said. "I'm sure Byron would love to see the planes."

"It'll mean an early start on Saturday morning. I suggest you and Byron come to my house on Friday and stay over."

Byron and I arrived at Dave's house in Swanley on Friday evening. With Natasha's help, Dave had been busy making a casserole for dinner. The tantalising aroma welcomed us as we came in. He proudly showed me his new dining room furniture that had recently been delivered.

"It fits in your dining room so well," I told him.

He took me through to his lounge. "Here's the three-piece suite you helped me to choose."

I gazed around, genuinely impressed by the transformation of his home. "You've done an incredible job, Dave. The new furniture and the decor, everything looks marvellous."

He grinned. "I've enjoyed changing the house to reflect my tastes. It feels more like my home now."

After a satisfying dinner, we tucked the children into bed. Dave had prepared the double bed in the spare room for Byron and me to share, while Natasha had her own single bedroom.

Then we relaxed with a coffee, chatting and enjoying the cosy atmosphere of Dave's lounge.

I walked over to a display case to admire Dave's miniature toy soldiers arranged in a battle scene. You've done a good job of painting these soldiers," I commented.

Dave smiled. "I like to give them the correct regimental colours on their uniforms, but it's very fiddly as they're so small. I've got loads of different regiments. It's a hobby I really enjoy. Byron shows a lot of interest in them, so I intend to leave them to him one day, in the fullness of time."

"That's very kind of you, Dave. I know Byron will really appreciate inheriting them."

"Now that I'm living here on my own, I've been considering taking in a lodger to help pay the bills," Dave said.

"That sounds like a practical idea. A lodger could also bring some additional company into your life," I remarked.

Dave nodded. "Maybe a nurse from the hospital who might help with the housework. I made some enquiries and was told several nurses are looking for digs."

I smiled. "Do I detect an ulterior motive in your choice of a pretty, young nurse as a lodger?"

Dave grinned. "Well, if I must share my house, I would much prefer a female companion," he admitted with a chuckle. "Hopefully, she wouldn't mind doing a spot of cleaning in return for a reduced rent."

"You've obviously thought about who you would like as a lodger. I hope it works out for you."

Dave made us a nightcap, and then we headed for our beds early, as we would need to be up at 5 a.m.

"I'll be collecting a Route Master 8 from the bus garage first thing in the morning," Dave said as we climbed the stairs. "There will be about twenty people coming with us."

Byron and I were pleasantly surprised when we were woken early the next morning by Dave, who came breezing into our bedroom carrying a tray laid out with our breakfast. This thoughtful gesture set us up for the day ahead.

"I'm off to the garage with Natasha to collect the bus and the other passengers. I'll be back for you two in about an hour."

"We'll be ready and waiting," I assured Dave.

In less than an hour, a red double-decker bus pulled up in front of Dave's house. We eagerly hurried out and climbed aboard. Dave introduced us to the others, who were his work colleagues and their families. With Dave at the wheel, we set off on our journey to the Lakenheath

31

U.S. Air Base in Suffolk. Natasha, Byron, and I squeezed onto the seat behind the driver's cab so that Natasha could watch her dad drive the bus.

On reaching Lakenheath, we joined a lengthy queue of traffic, all eager to enter the U.S. Air Base on their open day. Dave expertly parked the bus in a designated area on the airfield. We then climbed to the top deck of the bus, where we were treated to breathtaking views of the planes taxiing on the runways, their powerful engines roaring before they gracefully took off, circled around and then landed.

We all spent an exhilarating day watching the various planes perform aerial acrobatics in the sky. The deafening roar of the engines was overwhelming, especially if we happened to be standing directly behind an aircraft during take-off when we felt the ground shake beneath our feet.

We were shown inside a Nimrod, bristling with technical equipment. The engineers diligently worked in front of panels of instruments. We caught a glimpse of a sleek Blackbird in a hangar, but we didn't see it brought out on show.

The irresistible aroma of barbecued burgers wafted through the air, tempting us to indulge in the delicious snack. The burger, dipped in a delectable barbecue sauce, had an excellent flavour. The Americans certainly knew the art of grilling a scrumptious hamburger, and we couldn't resist returning for more.

Back at the bus, I took photos of Byron and Natasha's playful antics as they took turns sitting in the driver's seat, ringing the bell and pretending to drive the bus.

Once everyone had returned and boarded the bus, Dave drove us all home at the end of a delightful day on the American airbase. Both the children had tired themselves out. I thanked Dave for such a fantastic, memorable day and then brought Byron home.

As May drew to a close, Joan rang me, sounding excited. She and Cyril had found a four-bedroom executive house to rent in the charming market town of Reepham.

"It's only temporary until we take over a business," Joan explained. "While we're looking for a business, I've decided to put my name down with an employment agency in Norwich. I'm hoping to do some office work as the money will be useful, what with the rent to find for the new house once we've moved in. I think Stella and Mick will be pleased to have their house to themselves again. I expect Stella will have ideas for redecorating the small third bedroom as a nursery, ready for the baby's arrival."

"Is there any news yet from Stella about a baby?" I asked.

"No, but I'm sure, after Mick, I'll be the next to know if there was one on the way. Once we've settled in, you must come and see the new house. I can't wait to show it to you!"

I told Joan all about the air show and my ongoing search for a suitable business. After hanging up, I couldn't help wondering whether they had made the right decision to rent what was obviously an expensive house.

On the 9th of June, Maggie Thatcher won a landslide victory to secure her second term in office with a Tory government. Thanks to her, after over thirty years of renting, my parents were able to purchase their house under Maggie's controversial 'right to buy' scheme, which allowed council tenants to buy their homes at a discount. This scheme was a game-changer for my parents, giving them a sense of stability and ownership they had never experienced before.

The age of video games was advancing quickly. Despite being won over by the new Atari games, Byron still enjoyed playing the original black-and-white tennis game that plugged into the television. Each player had a bat, and the ball pinged from side to side across the screen until one scored by hitting the ball past their opponent's bat.

I had treated him to one of these games for his tenth birthday. However, since he had experienced the more exciting Atari games, I could guess what would be on his Christmas list.

For the time being, we enjoyed competing against each other, playing the tennis game. The television sat on top of a unit of white furniture that stood against the lounge wall.

Tia, being a playful kitten, always wanted to be part of the action. She would sit beside the television screen, her paw ready to swat at the ball as it darted back and forth. Her playful interruptions often led to missed shots and lost points. Still, we didn't mind because Tia was obviously enjoying herself, and her antics always made us smile.

The following week, I was thrilled to receive details in the post about a pet shop for sale in Sidcup. I had been eagerly hoping for a pet shop to come up for sale, and now, my dream shop was available. The prospect of owning a pet shop, a business with substantial profit margins, had always excited me, so I promptly made an appointment to view it the next day, thrilled at the thought that my search could be over. My dream could soon become a reality.

I found the double-fronted shop in a small parade of shops on Station Road in Sidcup, not far from the High Street. I stood outside, gazing at the frontage. According to the details, a large flat was spread over two floors upstairs with a sitting tenant. It had a sizeable picture window above the shop door. To the left of the shop, on the corner, was a hardware shop, and on the right was a gents haberdashers.

The pet shop was aptly named Flights because it stocked a wide variety of birds. I realised that running a pet shop would be challenging, especially managing the inventory and dealing with animal health issues. I took a deep breath and opened the door to what might be my new vocation.

As I stepped inside, the doorbell jangled, and I was immediately enveloped in a welcoming cacophony of noise. Guinea pigs were squeaking, budgies were chirping, canaries were shrilling, love birds and finches were cheeping, and cockatiels and a parrot were screeching. The shop was a good size, with the far side devoted to gardening requisites.

The owner, a friendly lady who I guessed was in her late thirties, introduced herself as Anne. She came out from behind the counter at the rear of the shop, shook my hand, and offered to show me around. Her warm smile and the lively, inviting atmosphere of the shop immediately put me at ease.

Large bags of corn and feed stood on the shop floor to one side in front of the counter. Anne pointed out the various contents of maize, wheat, and pony nuts; layer pellets and chicken meal; rabbit pellets, sunflower seeds, and peanuts. I loved the wonderful aroma of the feeds permeating the shop, mingling with the smell of hay, straw, and sawdust. The shelves on the side wall were filled with cages of various animals and an assortment of birds. A central shelving unit divided off the pet section from the gardening section of the shop, showcasing a wide selection of products.

Anne led me through the gardening section into a broad passageway with shelves where colourful cold-water fish swam in several aquariums. She pointed out the different species of goldfish, including fantails in various colours, comets, colourful shubunkins and black moors. There was also a vivarium containing a grass snake and another with tiny terrapins clambering over rocks or swimming in shallow pools.

At the end of the passageway, we passed through a plastic strip blind into a gloomy storeroom. One small dingy window offered the only natural light, set in a corner above a deep sink with a single draining board. Anne's desk filled a recess in the opposite corner beside a fireplace, now blocked off and no longer used. Shelving took up most of the remaining space.

Anne pointed out a bench, explaining that this was where the fresh meat, which arrived once a week, was cut up, weighed, and packed before being frozen and where name tags were engraved.

A door on the far side opened into a back room filled with cages on shelves. "These are our breeding animals," Anne explained. "Except for that black rabbit, which is Linda's own pet. Linda is my assistant - she's out at the moment. She's hoping the new owner will keep her on. Do you have any experience of running a pet shop?"

Despite my lack of experience in the pet business, I was filled with a strong desire to learn. "I'm certain I could quickly adapt," I said, striving to convey more confidence than I felt.

Anne smiled. "You'd find Linda very helpful if you decided to take on this shop. She knows how it runs."

I felt a sense of familiarity as I gazed around at the rabbits, guinea pigs, hamsters, gerbils, and mice. Having grown up with most of these animals as pets, being around them now made me feel right at home.

Returning to the storeroom, Anne led me through a door into a rear passage where the straw, hay, and sawdust were stacked on the floor.

At the far end, a door opened onto a small rear yard. The opposite end of the passage had another door leading back into the shop.

Outside, the yard had sufficient room to park a car. A metal staircase led up to the first-floor flat. Near the stairs, the outside toilet nestled inconspicuously in a corner.

Back in the storeroom, I asked Anne if I could borrow her accounts to check the figures. She went over to her desk and brought me her ledger.

"The profit margins are excellent, mostly around fifty per cent," she informed me. "You're welcome to take this home and browse through it." She could tell I was definitely interested in the shop. My excitement was evident in my eyes. I could easily visualise myself working here, with Linda to guide me until I found my feet.

As I returned home with my head in the clouds, I hoped I had finally found the right shop. I spent the evening perusing the accounts, which looked quite impressive, but I was aware that I was no accountant. I realised the importance of a second opinion from someone whose heart wasn't ruling their head. I immediately rang Dave and asked for his help, knowing I could rely on him to give me some sound advice.

Dave arrived the following evening, eager to hear about the pet shop. I was happy to talk about it over a cup of tea as we sat in the lounge.

Dave also had some news. "I've advertised for a lodger, and there's been some interest already. A nurse is coming to see the house at the weekend."

I was pleased for Dave. "That's just what you need. I hope she turns out to be the right lodger for you."

Dave took the pet shop ledger home, promising to scrutinise it carefully. "I'll return it to you next week; then, maybe, I'll be able to tell you all about my new lodger," he said as he was leaving.

The following week, on Wednesday evening, Dave arrived to return the pet shop ledger. We sat in the lounge, discussing the business accounts over coffee.

"I've studied the figures very carefully, and I must say, they look pretty good to me," Dave declared. "Not that I'm an expert in bookkeeping," he added.

"So you think this could be a viable venture?" I asked.

"The profit margins are very impressive. I see a great potential for success if you continue along the same lines as the current owner."

I felt relieved and pleased by Dave's optimistic assessment, so I told him of my idea. "I've been thinking about ways to expand and improve the business. At the moment, they only stock cold-water fish. I'm considering converting part of the storeroom into an area to house tropical fish. It's a large enough room to divide in order to accommodate the extra fish tanks, and I'm sure tropical fish would be popular."

Dave grinned. "Sounds like a great idea, although carrying out the necessary alterations and stocking up with the extra fish will probably be expensive."

I sighed. "Yes, you're right. I'll need to arrange a bank loan if I buy this shop because my redundancy money will only pay for the shop, not the stock."

"There's always some risk involved with running your own business, but I'm confident you'll be fine," Dave reassured me.

"I really appreciate your opinion, Dave. I'll contact the estate agent in the morning and arrange to meet him for a chat."

"By the way, that nurse liked my house, so she should be moving in as my lodger fairly soon."

"What's not to like? I know she'll be very comfortable sharing your home," I assured him.

Dave stood up to leave. "Having been married, I don't really enjoy living alone, so I'll be glad of the company. Perhaps I'll have help with the housework, too," he added with a smile.

"You did mention coming to an arrangement where she pays less rent in return for keeping the house tidy," I reminded him.

"Yes, I did, so I might suggest that to her," Dave said.

The next morning, I rang the Gibraltar estate agent marketing the pet shop and made an appointment for that afternoon.

I found the small office tucked away on a side street in the nearby town of Gravesend. The office had an unimpressive frontage. Inside, a young lady sat typing at a desk. She paused and smiled as I entered. I explained that

I had an appointment, so she picked up the telephone and spoke into it briefly.

Then she stood up. "Would you follow me, please," she said, opening a door and leading me along a passage to another door at the far end. She knocked and entered, announcing: "Your two o'clock appointment is here, Mr Davidson."

A dark-haired man in his late thirties with a swarthy complexion stood up behind his desk and extended his hand, greeting me with a warm smile. "Please, call me John," he said, shaking my hand. He seemed reluctant to let it go. As I sat down in the chair opposite him, I noticed a photo on his desk of a heavily made-up lady with bleached hair holding a small white dog. He saw me looking at the picture.

"Ah, that's my wife with our dog," he informed me. "I sometimes think she loves that dog more than she does me," he added with a laugh.

I felt a little ill at ease under his intense gaze. It was as if his eyes were undressing me. I quickly explained that I was interested in the pet shop at Sidcup, but I would need to arrange a bank loan.

"That shouldn't be a problem," he assured me. "I can organise that; I'll take the shop off the market and make an appointment with the manager of Lloyds Bank. I'll accompany you to the interview, although it should be a mere formality. However, you will need some figures to show him. Do you have any other form of income to boost the shop's income?"

I was surprised by his question and shook my head. Then I thought of Tia. "Well, I'm hoping to start breeding Persian cats next year, but I doubt that will impress a bank manager."

"Nonsense!" John exclaimed. "We need to make your income look as good as possible. Roughly how much do you expect to make a year from cat-breeding?"

I had no idea. "I haven't given it any thought," I admitted, wondering why John wanted to include the cat breeding, which was still only a pipe dream.

"Not to worry – I'll put some figures down on paper just to keep the bank manager happy," he said, making some notes. "Will this be a joint business venture with your husband?"

"No, I'm divorced. I intend to run the shop on my own. However, I might keep the current assistant on to help me."

John's eyes lit up. "So, you're divorced. Do you live alone?"

I felt he was being unnecessarily inquisitive. "I live with my son," I said and stood up to leave. "You've got my phone number. Let me know when you've made an appointment with the bank manager."

John jumped up and hurried over to me. I thought he would shake my hand, but he put his arm around my shoulders instead. "I shall look forward to our next meeting," he said, squeezing my shoulder. I instinctively pulled away from him, feeling uncomfortable. He was far too familiar, crossing a line that should not have been crossed.

John realised he had overstepped the mark. "I'm sorry. It's my Mediterranean blood. I'm from Gibraltar – hence the name of my agency." I got the impression that he considered himself God's gift to women. His arrogant behaviour made me uneasy, and I realised I would need to be constantly on guard around him. I left, wondering how his secretary coped with his amorous ways, or perhaps she didn't mind.

Two days later, I received a call from John, the estate agent. He had made the appointment for 11 a.m. the next morning. He arranged to collect me and drive us to the bank.

John arrived early the following day, catching me off guard. When I opened the door, he greeted me with a broad smile and strode in without waiting to be invited, clutching a portfolio of papers. His assertive presence immediately set me on edge, making it difficult for me to feel at ease in my own home.

"I want to show you the set of figures I've put together for the bank manager," he said, leading the way into the lounge. John sat on the sofa and spread the papers on the coffee table, forcing me to sit uncomfortably close to him in order to study the figures.

I read through them and then gasped in amazement. "These numbers suggest a thriving cat-breeding business, making a profit of £3,000 a year!" I exclaimed, unable to hide my surprise.

"Oh, these are just projected figures," John explained offhandedly. "We want to impress the bank manager so that he'll have no qualms about lending you the money."

It was downright dishonest, but John assured me it was an accepted practise. He quickly replaced the papers in the folder.

"As we've got some time to spare, why don't you show me around your lovely bungalow? Being an estate agent, I have a consuming interest in properties."

I hesitated, unsure of his real motives. He stood up and walked out into the hall. "Ah, I see your kitchen is along here," he said, striding down the hall. "You have plenty of space and have even extended out the back, creating a separate dining room."

"Yes, although It's not quite finished yet. With the two bedrooms, this bungalow is big enough for me and my son," I said.

"And are you going to show me your bedroom?" John asked with a cheeky grin. His comment sent a shiver down my spine and made me question his intentions.

"I think we ought to be going. I'll just fetch my handbag." I hurried into my bedroom, and John, showing no scruples, quickly followed me.

"Your boudoir!" he exclaimed. "What a comfortable-looking double bed." He came around the bed towards me. "We've got plenty of time; there's no rush," he said, placing his hands on my shoulders. "How about we have a bit of fun on the bed?" He pulled me towards him and tried to kiss me.

I recoiled from his touch. "No, John. I'm not interested in that kind of fun," I said firmly. I quickly ducked away and side-stepped around him. "Behave yourself," I added sharply. "You're a married man."

He shook his head. "My wife is a bit of a cold fish. I don't think she cares much about me anymore."

"That's no excuse for you to come on to me," I said.

"You're a lovely lady. Do you blame me for getting carried away?" He lunged towards me again, so I ran around the bed and out into the hall.

"It's time we left," I said over my shoulder and hurried out the front door.

He collected his portfolio and then caught up with me on the drive. "OK - you win," he said. "Let's head for this meeting and get your loan approved."

The meeting went remarkably smoothly, although I did find it somewhat nerve-racking. John had instructed me to go along with whatever he told the bank manager. However, I felt uncomfortable agreeing that the figures were accurate.

The bank manager's suggestion to hire an accountant for my VAT returns was a practical one. I felt relieved once the meeting was over and the loan had been approved.

John drove me home, but when we arrived, I made sure he stayed in his car and just dropped me off. I didn't fancy being chased around my bedroom again by a randy estate agent.

"It'll take a while for the sale to go through," he told me as I alighted. "I'll keep you informed as things progress."

"You've got my number, so just ring me if there's any news," I said firmly. I didn't want John turning up uninvited on my doorstep.

The next day, I drove to Sidcup to return Anne's ledger and tell her the good news that I intended to buy her shop. Being a Saturday, the shop was busy with a queue of customers waiting to be served. Linda was there, weighing out dog biscuits. I guessed she was in her late teens. Meanwhile, Anne was around the corner in the passageway, helping a customer choose some fish from an aquarium.

I waited patiently for the queue to be served. Linda was an attractive girl with short dark hair and a ready smile. She seemed very competent at her job. As she served the customers, a parrot perched on her shoulder, playfully tweaking her hair with its large beak.

Once the customers had all been served, Anne greeted me and was thrilled when I told her of my decision to buy her shop. She introduced me to Linda, and I explained that I was considering keeping her on to help run the shop when I took over.

This news pleased Linda immensely. "I'll make us all a cup of tea to celebrate," she declared and hurried off to the storeroom with the parrot still perched on her shoulder.

I mentioned to Anne the trouble I had experienced with the randy estate agent.

She laughed. "Oh, John's pretty harmless. When he came here to take the particulars on the shop, he ended up chasing me around the storeroom!"

"No!" I gasped, a little shocked at Anne's unexpected revelation about John's behaviour.

"He made the excuse that it's his hot Mediterranean blood!"

"Yes, that's what he told me," I said. "He's got a right cheek!"

Linda appeared with three mugs of tea and then introduced me to Pedro. "He's a blue-fronted Amazon

43

parrot," she explained. "He's not for sale – he stays with the shop. Nearly everyone in Sidcup knows Pedro. He's a right character, but he hates men for some unknown reason – he was once probably badly treated by a man. He can even crack Brazil nuts with his powerful beak."

"I can easily believe that!" I exclaimed. "He's very handsome - does he talk?"

"Oh, yes. Pedro has quite a wide repertoire."

"He even says, 'Hello, Ann'," Anne said with a grin. "It's lucky we've got the same name."

Linda held her hand up, and Pedro stepped onto it. She carefully placed him on my shoulder. I felt uneasy, knowing his beak was on a level with my eyes, especially as he didn't know me.

Linda could see I was nervous. "Pedro is fine with women," she reassured me. "He looks quite content, sitting on your shoulder."

"I think it's time Pedro went back in his cage," Anne told Linda. Linda presented her hand to Pedro, and he stepped on it again. Once back on the perch in his cage, Pedro started showcasing his various phrases. "What's the mat?" he kept repeating.

"That's short for 'What's the matter?'," Anne explained.

Pedro switched to "Come on" and "Hello, Ann" and then made a noise, imitating a Trimphone. His ability to mimic sounds was amazing.

I couldn't help laughing at his antics. Pedro immediately gave an infectious, loud belly laugh, rocking to and fro on his perch. This made me laugh even more. The more I laughed, the more Pedro laughed. "Oh, I can see we'll have a great time with Pedro to keep us entertained," I said.

"He also does police sirens and wolf whistles," Anne said. "I'm sure you could teach him some new phrases. Fortunately, he doesn't swear, which makes him more valuable than parrots that do swear."

Some more customers entered the shop, so I said goodbye and left, looking forward to an enjoyable new line of work.

Monday morning, I was pleasantly surprised to receive a letter from Keith, my former employer at Intertruck. He had been the managing director, and the computer had been his pet project, so I had enjoyed a close working relationship with him.

He emigrated to Florida with his family shortly before Intertruck closed. He had kindly invited me and Byron to visit him for a holiday at his home in Florida. However, I was certain his wife wouldn't have approved of me turning up at her house, so I politely declined his offer.

Now, he was writing to tell me about the business he had bought, making office furniture. He was disillusioned with his staff, saying they weren't a patch on the staff at Intertruck. He discovered some employees were stealing his stock, so he was forced to call in the sheriff to deal with the problem.

He ended his letter by again inviting me and Byron to take a holiday in Clearwater with him and his family. I replied, telling Keith all about the difficulty I had searching for the right business, and described the pet shop I planned to buy. I commiserated with him on the problem he had with his staff. However, I didn't commit to taking a holiday in Florida.

The exhilarating prospect of my new business venture brought back memories of the last time I had considered becoming self-employed. In 1968, I was excited about creating bespoke clothes and transforming an old caravan into a mobile dress shop. My zany boyfriend, Ralph, enthusiastically endorsed this seemingly crazy idea. Although he had been my boyfriend for over a year, I had never considered him more than just a good friend.

The enormity of the task soon dawned on me. I realised it was totally impractical, so I gave up on the scheme.

Now, I was keen to hear Ralph's opinion, and hopefully get his approval of my new business venture. With this in mind, I set out to track him down. When we last spoke, he worked in the computer department at Southampton University.

I rang the university the next day, and after being transferred around, I eventually heard Ralph's familiar voice on the other end of the phone. He sounded genuinely pleased to hear from me, which was a relief. The last time we saw each other, when I was working at Intertruck, we parted with a bit of tension in the air. Ralph had seemed to want me exclusively to himself. He had been keen for us to get back together again. However, I decided it wouldn't work, partly because I had detected some jealousy from Ralph towards Byron. Now, his warm response reassured me that our friendship was still intact.

We chatted briefly, and he sounded intrigued when I mentioned the pet shop I intended to buy. He was full of questions and seemed genuinely interested in my plans.

"I'm coming to Kent at the weekend to visit my parents," he said. "How about I pop in to see you while I'm there?"

"That's a great idea; then we can catch up properly with our news," I told him, pleased that we would meet once again.

"My seven-year-old son will be with me – you won't mind, will you?" he asked, sounding a little anxious.

"Of course, I won't mind," I reassured him. I wanted Ralph to feel comfortable bringing his son. I was looking forward to meeting him.

Saturday morning, I waited nervously for Ralph's arrival. Byron was at his nan and grandad's house, playing with his friends.

Late morning, the doorbell rang. I found Ralph's familiar lanky figure standing on my doorstep, looking a little ragged around the edges and needing a shave. His mop of fair, curly hair was more unkempt and wilder than usual. A shy young boy stood beside him. I invited them indoors.

"This is my older son, Kevin," Ralph said as they sat down in the lounge. "He's staying with me for the weekend." Ralph had been married long enough to have two sons. However, the marriage hadn't lasted, and now he was divorced, living alone in a three-bedroom semi in the suburbs of Southampton. He rented out one of his rooms to a university student.

I made some drinks and invited them to stay for lunch. Kevin plucked up the courage to ask if he could play in the back garden, so I gave him Byron's football to kick around.

Ralph was eager to hear all about the pet shop. I showed him the details I had received from the estate agent. He read them with interest and agreed that the shop sounded like a good investment.

I also introduced him to Tia Maria. "I'm hoping to breed from her next year," I said as I picked her up and handed her to Ralph. He gave her a cuddle, and she purred contentedly.

"We once planned to breed rough collies," Ralph reminded me.

"Yes, I remember how excited we were about the prospect of raising those beautiful dogs together," I reminisced with a hint of wistfulness in my voice. "Then, we had a change of plan and decided to emigrate to Australia instead. You took advantage of the £10 assisted passage to travel to Australia first in search of work." This important decision was a turning point when our dreams and plans diverged.

Ralph sighed. "That was a long time ago. We were called Ten Pound Poms by the Aussies. For some reason, our plans never materialised." He tactfully didn't mention my change of heart when I decided Australia, with its poisonous snakes and spiders, wasn't for me.

47

Ralph went on to speak about his bond with Kevin. "We are very close; he's been through a lot. He had to undergo several operations on his hands because he was born with webbed fingers. Fortunately, the operations were a complete success." His love and concern for Kevin was evident.

Ralph's eyes lit up with enthusiasm as he changed the subject and told me about the forty-foot ocean-going catamaran he had painstakingly built, which now rested in the tranquil waters of Southampton's harbour. His dedication to the project was admirable. I had witnessed its humble beginnings, a mere dream taking shape in Ralph's back garden.

"I'm still fitting it out - it's taking much longer than I originally envisaged. Once it's ready, I intend to take some long voyages. I'm hoping my sons will want to come with me." This boat had clearly become a significant part of Ralph's life.

I prepared some lunch, but Ralph insisted all he and Kevin wanted was tinned rice pudding, which they had brought with them. He reminded me that he was still vegetarian. However, the last time we met, in 1975, he had quickly ditched his newly formed vegetarian ideals when he saw the succulent chicken I had cooked for a picnic.

Over lunch, Ralph described his goodwill gesture of feeding the protestors camped at Greenham Common, a site of significant anti-nuclear protests. "I really admire what those women are doing, so I like to help out. I take my van, packed with food and drinks, whenever I get some free time."

"You certainly keep yourself busy," I declared. I tried including Kevin in our conversation, but he seemed withdrawn and shy, quietly eating his rice pudding. "Are you still living at the same address in Southampton?" I asked Ralph.

"Yes, it's a comfortable house, as you know from when you visited me in the seventies." Ralph paused and hesitated, then continued. "I've got a girlfriend, now. Well, she's really just a friend, but she seems to be infatuated with me. She likes to spend her spare time helping me fit out the boat."

"I'm glad to hear that," I said.

"The trouble is, she's only fifteen and still at school," Ralph confessed, his voice tinged with concern.

"What!" I gasped. "You're old enough to be her father."

"Yes, I realise it's far from an ideal situation. She is so sweet and innocent; I don't have the heart or will to send her away because I know it would devastate her."

I was shocked by Ralph's revelation. I could only hope the girl would come to her senses as she matured.

After Ralph and Kevin had left, I searched for Tia but couldn't find her. The thought that she might have escaped outside, probably when Kevin came indoors after playing in the garden, was unbearable. He wouldn't have known that she wasn't allowed outside.

I walked down the garden, calling her. She had never been outside, so I hoped she wouldn't wander too far away. But my calling was in vain; there was no sign of her. I was overwhelmed with a sense of loss and devastation.

I collected Byron and brought him home. He helped me to search the surrounding area, calling Tia's name. I felt as if history was repeating itself. I was haunted by the memory of losing my Siamese kitten in 1977 after allowing her into the garden.

I dreaded having to tell Debbie that I had lost my beloved Tia. I couldn't sleep that night; I was so worried. I got up early the next morning to continue searching for her, but my efforts proved fruitless.

On Monday morning, I placed a notice in the local newsagent's window with a picture of Tia, desperately hoping it would catch someone's eye and bring her back to me.

Returning home, I rang an accountant Anne had recommended and arranged for him to do my VAT returns once I was managing the pet shop.

The days passed agonisingly slowly for me as I waited for some response from my advert, but there was none. No one had any news of Tia, and my hope of seeing her again was fading fast.

Thursday, Byron arrived home from school and found me busy making our evening meal. He went into the garden but soon came dashing back, looking excited.

"Mum, I think I heard Tia. I was down the garden and called her name. I'm sure I heard a faint mew."

I hurried into the garden, my heart pounding, hoping he was right. Byron led me to the far end, and I called Tia's name. Then, I heard a mew, barely audible, that filled me with overwhelming relief and delight. I felt sure it was Tia. I could hardly dare hope she had been found.

"That sounds like Tia answering me," I told Byron. I managed to peer over the high fence into my neighbour's garden and saw a shed with a padlock on the door. The mews were coming from inside this shed.

"Oh, Byron, she's probably been locked in that shed since Saturday. That's five days! The poor thing must be starving. Why on earth didn't she mew in answer to our calls before today?"

"Perhaps she thought it was a game, but now that she's starving, she's decided the game isn't fun anymore."

We quickly ran next door to Mrs French's chalet bungalow and rang her doorbell, impatient to rescue Tia. Mrs French was a friendly divorcee who lived with her teenage son. She was amazed when I explained Tia's predicament and was eager to help.

"I haven't been down to my shed since Saturday. That must have been when your kitten slipped inside and hid up."

We all hurried down the garden, and Mrs French unlocked the shed door. There stood Tia, looking pleased

50

to see us. She didn't appear to be any the worse for her first adventure in the big wide world. I scooped her up in my arms, and she purred loudly as we all fussed over her. It was a moment of sheer joy.

"I'm so glad we found her safe and well," Mrs French declared as we returned to her kitchen. She wanted me to stop and chat, but I was impatient to take Tia home and give her some much-needed food and a drink. I was thankful I wouldn't need to tell Debbie about Tia's disappearance.

That night, Tia slept on my bed because I didn't want to let her out of my sight. She curled up next to me, purring contentedly. I was so pleased to get her back, and just in time before a predicted heatwave arrived the following day.

The 15th of July proved to be a scorcher, with temperatures soaring as high as thirty-three degrees in London. I felt deeply relieved that Tia was back home, safe and sound, before the intense heat struck.

Chapter Three

Taken Too Soon

Dave rang on Saturday evening to invite me and Byron to accompany him and Natasha on a trip to Norfolk the following weekend. "A mate of mine has a good fridge/freezer he no longer needs. When I rang Joan yesterday evening, I happened to mention the fridge/freezer, and she immediately said they would like to have it. I'll need to hire a van for the weekend to get it to their house."

I was excited at the prospect of visiting Joan and Cyril and seeing their new house at Reepham. It had been far too long since Byron and I had last seen them.

Dave and Natasha arrived in a white rental van early Saturday afternoon to collect me and Byron. We drove to a nearby town to pick up the fridge/freezer from a maisonette. Dave and his mate managed to carry it to the van, and then we were on our way.

The warm, settled weather put us in high spirits, and we were eagerly looking forward to a wonderful weekend in Norfolk.

We drew up outside an imposing detached house on a quiet road in Reepham. Joan's face lit up with excitement as she rushed out to greet us, followed by Cyril. Dave and

Cyril wasted no time unloading the fridge/freezer and storing it in the garage while Joan ushered us indoors, eager to show us around.

The spacious house, with four double bedrooms, exuded a homely atmosphere. Downstairs, the hall led to a large, comfortable lounge, a separate dining room and a well-equipped kitchen.

The garden was a lush green space with a variety of flowers and a well-maintained lawn. Joan made us all drinks and we sat in the lounge chatting while Byron and Natasha explored the back garden.

I told Joan and Cyril about the pet shop I was in the process of buying. They were pleased I had finally found a profitable shop, whereas they were still searching for their elusive ideal business.

"We're all set up for a barbecue this evening," Joan declared excitedly. "Stella is home from Saudi, so she will be joining us."

"Once Stella arrives, I'll light the barbecue," Cyril said. "Then we can pop along to the pub for a quick drink while the barbecue fires up."

Just then, the doorbell chimed. "I expect that's Stella, now," Joan said, jumping to her feet. She went to answer the door and returned with Stella, who was overjoyed to see us all. I hadn't seen Stella since she moved to Norfolk with Mick before they started working in Saudi Arabia.

Stella was a very attractive girl with shoulder-length, wavy blonde hair. She was a couple of years younger than her brother, Stuart, and had been in the same class as my brother at junior school.

We all greeted her with fond hugs. Stella explained that Mick had stayed on, working in Saudi Arabia, while she had come home to undergo a fertility test at the hospital.

Cyril went outside to get the barbecue started on the patio.

"I've brought corn on the cob wrapped in foil, ready for the barbecue," Stella announced. "And I've made a trifle for dessert."

"And I've prepared a picnic for tomorrow," Joan said. "As the weather is so lovely, we thought it would be a good idea to spend the day on the beach at Hunstanton." The children were thrilled at this news.

Dave beamed with pleasure. "That's a fantastic idea." He always had a healthy appetite, so he fully appreciated all the food being prepared.

Once Cyril had lit the barbecue, we all took a leisurely stroll to the local pub. As it was a lively Saturday evening, the pub was crowded.

We stood beside the jukebox, enjoying a cold beer while the children had squash. We found talking over the general hubbub and the music blaring from the jukebox difficult, but it didn't dampen our spirits. We stayed for one drink and then headed back to the house.

The evening was bathed in a warm golden glow from the setting sun, and the delicious aroma of barbecued food wafted across the back garden. The barbecue was a great success. Joan had prepared various dishes to accompany the meat and corn on the cob.

We sat outside with cold drinks, the warm evening air filled with our laughter and lively conversations. Whenever Dave and Cyril got together, they sparked off each other with their quick repartees, each trying to outwit the other.

Byron and Natasha yelled excitedly when they discovered a large toad in the flower border. They immediately called for Joan to come and see it, unsure if it was a toad or a frog. Joan explained the difference with her usual patience and confirmed that it was indeed a toad, easily identified by its brown skin covered with warty lumps.

Just as the children were about to head upstairs to bed, the doorbell rang, announcing Stuart's unexpected arrival.

His sudden appearance was a pleasant addition to the evening, catching us all by surprise. Byron, in particular, was overjoyed to see his dad, whom he hadn't seen in a long time.

Stuart now lived and worked in Fakenham, not too far from Reepham. He seemed discontent with his job at the private mental hospital and hinted at a potential job change.

Although Stuart and Dave had grown up together as best friends, their lives had drifted apart in recent years. Stella hadn't seen much of her brother as she spent most of her time working in Saudi.

This evening, there was a heart-warming atmosphere as old friendships were rekindled, and the family was reunited once again, filling the room with warmth and nostalgia.

None of us gathered together there realised that tragedy would strike one of us in the next few days, affecting our lives forever.

"It's a pity you didn't let us know you intended to come over. Now, you've missed out on the barbecue 'cos we've eaten it all," Cyril remarked to Stuart with a wry grin. "If we'd known, we might have kept some food for you."

"I was working until 9 o'clock tonight, so I couldn't have got here any earlier," Stuart said. "I decided to come and see you all while you're here in Norfolk for the weekend."

After Stuart and Stella had left, we all retired to bed, eagerly looking forward to a fantastic day at the seaside on Sunday.

The next morning, after breakfast, I helped Joan pack the picnic hamper while Byron and Natasha scoured the garden for more toads. Dave was still in the bathroom as he was late getting up.

"Poor Dave was up most of the night, catching up with his paperwork as he's off to Greece tomorrow for a fortnight's holiday," Joan said. "I came downstairs at two o'clock in the morning and found him sitting at the dining room table, scribbling away. He complained of a headache, so I fetched him some tablets."

"Dave did mention he was off on holiday Monday morning. That's why he wanted to bring the fridge/freezer up here this weekend before he left for Greece," I said.

Joan sighed. "His job as manager of the bus garage really puts him under a lot of pressure. He needs this holiday to recharge his batteries."

"He's going to Greece with his mate, Terry, the manager of another bus garage," I said.

"If I remember correctly, you and Terry were an item about eighteen months ago," Joan remarked. Terry's name could still stir up painful memories. I had fallen hopelessly in love with him; however, I eventually discovered he wasn't the wonderful person I thought he was.

"No doubt you recall, Joan, how Terry and I first met at Stella's house when Dave invited Terry to your New Year's Eve party. Anyway, that's all in the past. Let's get the children and head off to Hunstanton. I'm really looking forward to a fun-filled day."

We all managed to cram into Cyril's estate car, packing everything we needed for the beach in the back. The sun shone down from a clear blue sky as we arrived at Hunstanton, known as Sunny Hunny, which was undoubtedly appropriate today.

We enjoyed a typical day on the beach, paddling in the surf and kicking a ball around. Dave bought buckets and spades from a stall, so we had a competition to see who could make the best sandcastle.

We picnicked on a blanket spread out on the sand. Joan had made a large delicious quiche with coleslaw, sausage rolls, sandwiches, and cake. A cool box kept the drinks refreshingly chilled.

Mid-afternoon, Dave treated everyone to ice creams. Eventually, it was time to pack up and head back to

Reepham at the end of a perfect day. Joan insisted we stay for tea before starting our journey back to Kent.

"I've got to drop Natasha off near Penny's sister's house," Dave said. "For some reason, Penny doesn't want me knocking on her sister's door, so she said she will wait at the corner of the road."

Once tea was over, Dave was keen to start the journey home. We thanked Joan and Cyril for a wonderful weekend and said our goodbyes before climbing aboard the van.

"I know Penny will be absolutely furious if I'm late taking Natasha back," he confided to me quietly so Natasha wouldn't hear. "These days, she flies off the handle at the slightest thing."

Unfortunately, the journey home was far from smooth. We encountered several delays, and I could sense Dave's tension mounting as the clock ticked past the nine o'clock deadline for returning Natasha.

We finally arrived nearly an hour late at the rendezvous on the corner of the road. Dave handed over Natasha and received a tirade of verbal abuse from Penny for keeping her waiting so long.

When Dave climbed back into the van, he was in a daze and didn't seem to know what he was doing after receiving such a dreadful lambasting from Penny with her temper tantrum. I felt sorry for poor Dave. It wasn't his fault that we were so late. On such a long journey, delays were inevitable. He didn't get an opportunity to justify his lateness, and Penny was in no mood to listen.

Dave had recovered his composure by the time he drew up outside my bungalow. "I'll be greatly relieved once the divorce is finalised and I can get on with my life," he declared, sounding weary but determined. His relationship with Penny had been strained for some time with frequent arguments. This incident was just another hurdle in their troubled marriage.

"Forget about Penny and make the most of your holiday," I told him as I helped a sleepy Byron down from the van. "I hope you enjoy yourself in Greece and get plenty of rest." It was clear to me that Dave needed a break from the stress and tension of his marriage.

Dave nodded, a glimmer of excitement in his eyes. "I'm really looking forward to this holiday. I'll send you a postcard," he promised with a wave, then drove away to return the rental van.

On Wednesday evening, Penny rang me unexpectedly. She didn't beat about the bush; she simply blurted out, "Dave is dead." Her voice was cold and matter-of-fact, devoid of any emotion.

"What!" I gasped in utter disbelief and shock, unable to comprehend her words. Dave was on holiday, enjoying himself. How could he possibly be dead? It just didn't make sense. I kept waiting for Penny to say she was joking, but the seriousness in her voice told me otherwise.

A vision flashed into my mind of Dave diving off a rock into the Aegean Sea and hitting his head on a submerged rock. "Did he have an accident?"

"No. It happened yesterday. Apparently, he suffered an aneurysm."

I was devastated. The news hit me like a ton of bricks. I found it difficult to accept that my dear friend Dave was gone. The thought of never again hearing his quick-witted humour and infectious laughter was unbearable. His death left a void in my life that I knew would never be filled.

"He complained of a terrible headache," Penny continued. "This turned out to be the fatal aneurysm."

I recalled Joan mentioning Dave's headache at the weekend and his confused state when he returned to the van after dropping off Natasha Sunday evening. "Would you like me to let Joan and Cyril know?" I asked, my mind turning to more practical matters.

"No. I'll call and tell them what has happened," Penny said firmly. "I'll let you know about the funeral arrangements once Dave's body is back in this country."

I hung up the phone and sat in a daze, my mind whirling from this dreadful news. Dave was only thirty-four – far too young to die. Both his parents had died relatively young from kidney disease, and now Dave had joined them, reunited in death. I felt concerned for Natasha, now left fatherless in the world. My heart went out to her.

I couldn't help wondering whether the lambasting Dave received from Penny on Sunday evening had speeded up his fatal brain haemorrhage. She hadn't sounded upset, just cold and practical. No doubt Penny would inherit everything since the divorce wasn't finalised. I knew Dave wouldn't have wanted Penny to benefit from his death after the appalling way she had treated him. Fate could be so cruel.

Meanwhile, life had to go on. I was busy getting Tia ready for her first show on Saturday. I bathed her and put her in a basket to dry her fur with the hairdryer. Then, I gave her coat a sprinkling of baby talcum powder, and brushed it thoroughly to remove the excess talc, leaving it soft and fluffy. I remembered to pay attention to the minute details, like removing the little tufts of fur on her ears to give them a neat, rounded shape, just as Debbie had shown me.

Preparing Tia for the upcoming show became a welcome distraction. The necessary daily routines of powdering and brushing her during the final week before the show helped me avoid dwelling too much on Dave's untimely demise.

The Kensington Kitten and Neuter Cat Club normally held its annual show at Kensington. However, the hall was being refurbished, so this year, it was being held down on the coast at Brighton. Debbie's husband was driving us all down there, along with another of Debbie's friends. It meant an early start on Saturday morning.

The day promised to be a scorcher, so I packed a picnic with plenty of food for everyone. I wore a black sundress as I was still mourning Dave's loss.

We all chipped in towards the cost of the petrol and arrived at the venue in plenty of time. The show was being held in a hotel just across the road from the beach. We joined the queue for vetting-in, a nerve-racking time when every cat and kitten was carefully checked by a vet before being allowed into the main hall.

I settled Tia in her pen on the regulation white blanket, along with a litter tray and water dish, also in white. Then, the hall was cleared, ready for the judging.

The results began to be displayed at around twelve noon. Byron and I were thrilled when Tia emerged victorious in every class I had entered her in. Mrs Ashford, a respected and seasoned judge, was responsible for the fair and thorough judging of all the classes. Tia's triumph over her two litter mates in the main open class was a moment of sheer joy, filling me with pride and happiness. It was a much-needed boost during a difficult time. Debbie was disappointed that her blue point kitten, Tiffany, could only manage third place, while the seal point girl, Kizzi, came second.

Debbie and her friends vanished at lunchtime, so Byron and I decided to make the most of the good weather by heading for the beach to savour our picnic in the warm sunshine. The cooling sea breeze, the sound of seagulls, and the sight of children playing in the sea all added to the enjoyment of our picnic.

In the afternoon, after the judging had finished, the general public was allowed into the hall to view the exhibits. I proudly took photos of Byron cuddling Tia beside her rosettes, which were displayed on her pen.

At the end of the afternoon, the climax of the show arrived, and the tension in the hall was noticeable as the

Best in Show was chosen - a handsome, long-haired smoke neuter. With the show coming to a close, it was time to pack up our things and return Tia to her basket.

On the journey home, I shared the extra salmon and cucumber sandwiches. They made a welcome snack at the end of an exhausting yet exciting day.

August arrived, and Ford's new Fiesta car and the new A prefix registration plates were launched. I still had my Dolomite car, but I realised I would need an estate car to do cash and carry once I took over at the pet shop.

Receiving a postcard from Dave was a totally unexpected surprise. The card was postmarked the 26th of July, the day he died. I was deeply touched by this poignant reminder that he had kept his promise to send me a postcard. I felt so grateful, knowing this was the last I would hear from him.

He wrote: "Made it! As I write this card, I am sitting on the balcony of our apartment overlooking the Aegean Sea, which is clear and blue! If you look on the map, we are on the Peloponnese (S.E. side of Athens). See you when I get back. DAVROS xxx"

As I read the postcard, I was overwhelmed by a profound sense of loss for my dear friend. Was it a mere stroke of luck, or could fate have urged Dave to write the card on the first day of his holiday? Otherwise, I would never have received this final message from him.

When the day of Dave's funeral arrived, I found myself in a heart-wrenching predicament. I had to choose to attend and face Terry or stay away. Joan had rung to say she couldn't get time off from her office work to travel down to Kent.

Her absence meant I wouldn't have the moral support I needed to face Terry. The thought of attending the funeral without her was daunting. I doubted whether I would be able to cope, so I finally made the painful decision not to go. It was a decision that weighed heavily on me. Still, I found comfort in the cherished memory of that wonderful last weekend when Dave, Natasha, Byron and I travelled to Norfolk and enjoyed the barbecue in the garden, followed by a fun day on the beach at Hunstanton with Joan and Cyril.

Dave was given a remarkable send-off, a testament to his impact on those around him. His coffin was placed on a Route Master 8 bus and bedecked with a wreath. It was the oldest bus still in London Transport service and made a fitting tribute to his love for the sturdy bus in which he had organised rallies and fund-raising events.

The local paper described how Dave died of a brain haemorrhage on the Greek Island of Poros, with the cremation taking place at Falconwood. But amidst all this, the news that a trust fund had been established for Natasha brought me some comfort. I recalled Dave promising to leave his toy soldiers to Byron, but I doubted whether Penny would fulfil Dave's wish.

Dave's dining room furniture had been bought on a weekly basis from my catalogue. However, he had only managed to make a few payments before his untimely death.

A woman from the catalogue company contacted me. She cheekily asked me to pay the outstanding balance on Dave's account because they didn't want to get embroiled in probate matters. I was shocked and appalled by their insensitivity at such a difficult time. I insisted it would have to go to probate, and they would receive their money from Dave's estate in due course. The woman had no option other than to reluctantly agree. I could tell from the icy tone of her voice that she was far from pleased with the situation, as if implying that Dave had done this on purpose!

By the 19th of August, temperatures had reached thirty degrees in London as the hot weather continued.

Towards the end of August, I received an excited phone call from Joan. "We've just viewed a supermarket at Thetford. It's in a small square of shops and has a good turnover. There are two flats on the first floor, so one could be rented out for extra income. Cyril is very keen, so we have decided to go ahead and buy it."

"That's marvellous news," I said, genuinely impressed by their decision. "I admire your courage in taking on such a venture. But I can't help being a little worried about the workload a supermarket might entail for the two of you."

I recalled Cyril's health scare a few years back and wondered whether this might prove to be more work than was good for him. Some years ago, Cyril had suffered a minor heart attack, making it crucial for him to avoid any extra work that could cause stress. I felt concerned that managing a supermarket might be too much at their time of life.

Joan shrugged off my worries. "We'll have several members of staff to help out with the work, so I'm sure we'll manage fine. My bookkeeping skills will be useful for doing the accounts, and Cyril plans to improve the deli and off-licence."

"It all sounds really exciting. I shall look forward to seeing the supermarket."

"It will be a few months before we can take over the shop. How is your pet shop coming along?"

I sighed. "Very slowly. I intend to visit the shop to check on how the sale is progressing."

"Before we are tied down, running our respective shops, I shall come down to Kent to visit you both," Joan declared. "We won't have a chance once we're busy in our shops."

"We'll look forward to seeing you," I told Joan and then hung up. Despite Joan's assurances, my worries remained about the amount of work they would be taking on, managing a supermarket. There would be far more work involved than running a delicatessen.

At the beginning of September, I decided to take another trip to the pet shop at Sidcup. I could simply ring the agent to find out how the sale was progressing, but I wanted to avoid a conversation with randy John. I preferred to get the latest update from Anne.

As I entered the shop, the welcoming aroma of feed and animals greeted me, along with the familiar symphony of bird songs and a wolf whistle from Pedro on his perch in his cage.

Linda looked pleased to see me. She hurried off to put the kettle on for tea. Anne finished serving a customer and then had time for a chat. She assured me that everything was moving along smoothly with the sale.

"These things always seem to take much longer than I expect – solicitors don't hurry themselves," she said. "John called in the other day with a progress report, but I think it was just an excuse to cadge a cup of tea as he happened to be in the area. He tried cornering me in the storeroom again, but I managed to escape his clutches. That man never knows when to quit!" Anne gave a laugh; she obviously regarded John's unwanted advances as just a bit of harmless fun. Pedro joined in with a belly laugh, rocking on his perch. His laughter was so infectious I couldn't help laughing at his antics.

Linda appeared from the storeroom with the tea, and I reassured her that I would definitely want her to stay at the shop. I felt confident we could work well together. Linda's eyes lit up with pleasure at my decision.

Anne told me about her other business venture. "Once the shop is sold, I'll have more time to devote to my breeding program. I breed St Bernard dogs, and now I'll be able to expand the business."

"They are gorgeous dogs, but I imagine they require a lot of care," I said.

Anne nodded and smiled. "Yes, they do. One sweep of their tail can clear the coffee table!"

She produced a book from under the counter and showed me a plethora of recipes for making the various bird feeds, plus hamster, gerbil, and mouse feeds. I was impressed by the sheer number of them.

The various mixtures for the birds were stored on a shelf in labelled jars above the bins of loose dog biscuits and hamster food.

Then she pulled out another book. "This is where I keep a record of all the coal orders for delivery, mainly during the winter months."

"You also supply coal?" I asked, my surprise evident in my voice.

Anne explained: "It's just a side-line. It's up to you whether you want to continue with it. Another side-line we offer is boarding animals when their owners go away on holiday. I had a batch of newly hatched ducklings and goslings that I managed to sell to the somewhat bemused locals on the understanding that I would board them when they went on holiday. Quite a few people have taken me up on that offer."

I smiled at the thought of ducks and geese waddling around the shop. "I had better honour your promise, else I won't be very popular with your customers."

"There's plenty of space in the back room for boarding, so it shouldn't be a problem," Anne assured me. "Just remember to give them a tub of water for a daily swim."

I hadn't fully appreciated just how diverse the work would be. It made me all the more keen to get involved in such a satisfying job. There was definitely no comparison between managing a computer and managing a pet shop. However, I was confident I would be equal to the challenge ahead of me, especially with Linda to assist me.

One evening the following week, Roger and Shelley surprised me with an unexpected visit. They were clearly brimming with some momentous news.

I quickly made some coffee and ushered them into the lounge. Shelley pulled out a paper from her handbag and handed it to me. It was a brochure from an estate agent detailing a property for sale.

"We've been to view this end-of-terrace house and decided to buy it!" Shelley exclaimed, her eyes sparkling with excitement.

I read through the paper. The picture showed a Victorian house on the corner of a road. Judging by the large picture window, it had once been a corner shop.

Roger and Shelley had been dating for many years, so it didn't come as a surprise that they wanted to move on with their relationship by buying a house together. My brother tended to be a stick in the mud, so I knew he would have given this new phase in their lives a lot of careful thought. However, I suspected that Shelley was the instigator in them buying a house.

On the 2nd of October, Neil Kinnock was elected as the new leader of the Labour Party, replacing Michael Foot. The party was undoubtedly hoping he would give Maggie a more challenging time during question time in the House of Commons, a prospect that excited Joan and Cyril. They were devout Labour supporters, especially Joan, who preferred Michael Foot to the Welshman Neil Kinnock. Their admiration for Michael Foot stemmed from his unwavering commitment to socialist principles. Joan loved nothing better than talking politics, weaving the subject into any conversation, often leading to lively debates.

Joan called me one evening and announced that she would visit us at the weekend, as she had promised. She would travel from Norfolk on a National Express coach, so we arranged to meet her in London on Saturday afternoon. Byron was on his half-term holiday, chuffed that he had no school for a week.

We caught the train to London, eager to meet Joan at Victoria coach station. As she stepped off the coach, we rushed over and threw our arms around her, hugging her. We were thrilled to see her again, and the feeling was clearly mutual.

We spent the afternoon at the Tower of London, fully immersing ourselves in its rich history and enjoying the sightseeing. This was followed by a scrumptious meal at a restaurant. Afterwards, Joan insisted on treating us to an entertaining evening at a West End show.

We headed to the Savoy Theatre on the Strand, excited to watch the intriguing play, 'Noises Off'. The play's surprise elements, cleverly woven into the plot, kept us on the edge of our seats, enjoying every moment.

Each seat was provided with a pair of opera glasses. Joan made good use of hers to see the performance better as our seats were off to one side of the stage.

On our way home on the train, Joan was surprised to discover she had absent-mindedly put the opera glasses in her handbag. "Oh, dear, if Cyril was here, he would tell me off for being scatterbrained," she declared with a laugh.

We arrived home late that night, and Joan insisted she would be fine sleeping on the settee in the lounge. I wanted to make her as comfortable as possible, so I made her a cosy bed to ensure she slept well.

We were all up early on Sunday morning. Joan suggested we accompany her back to Norfolk aboard the National Express coach. We were keen to do this, but before leaving, I rang my brother and asked him to take care of our cats while we were away.

Then we caught the train to London and boarded a bus to Victoria, where we caught the Norfolk-bound coach.

Cyril met us at Norwich bus station, looking pleased to see us. After exchanging warm hugs, he drove us home to Reepham. We realised this would be our last chance to share some quality time together before we each delved into our new business ventures.

Cyril had prepared a delectable meal for us. We relaxed and relished the delicious food while we caught up on our news.

Knowing Joan had to return to work on Monday morning, Cyril prepared a large pot of porridge and let it simmer on the stove overnight. We retired to bed, looking forward to waking up to the appetising aroma of a hot breakfast.

Cyril had an appointment at the solicitor's office in the morning. After our tasty breakfast, we said goodbye to him and caught a bus into Norwich. The bus took us on a long detour around the outlying villages, collecting passengers until it eventually arrived in Norwich city centre.

We parted near the bus station, and Joan headed for her office while Byron and I stopped at a bakery to buy some filled rolls for the journey before catching the coach back to London.

We sat near the rear of the coach, but before we had travelled many miles, we became aware of the acidic odour of vomit wafting up from the floor. A previous passenger had been sick, and the coach hadn't been cleaned properly between journeys. This made for a very unpleasant journey. The other seats were occupied, so we couldn't move to better seats. I'm never a good passenger on buses or coaches at the best of times, as I tend to suffer from travel sickness, although I have improved over the last few years. This situation wasn't helping me to overcome my own waves of nausea.

We eventually arrived home feeling tired from the long journey. Nonetheless, we both thoroughly enjoyed our weekend with Joan and Cyril.

The day of my takeover at the pet shop was slowly drawing nearer. My excitement was building, so I decided the time had come to bid farewell to my Dolomite and embrace a more practical estate car.

I scoured the classifieds in the local paper until I came across an Escort estate for sale in the nearby town of Northfleet.

I immediately called the garage advertising the car and arranged a viewing for the next day.

Unfortunately, I was met with a flat battery when I attempted to start the Dolomite. Undeterred, I walked to the end of my road and caught a bus instead. The uneventful, short journey took me straight to the garage.

A pristine, white Ford Escort estate car immediately caught my eye as I approached, parked on the forecourt next to a small office building.

Before I could inspect it, a good-looking young man emerged from the office, eager to greet me. He welcomed me with a smile, shook my hand and introduced himself as Doug. He was enthusiastic about the car's features and suggested I take it for a test drive.

As I manoeuvred the car, its familiar handling brought back a flood of fond memories. It wasn't just the Escort I had learned to drive and passed my test with in 1969. It was also my beloved Escort GT, a car I had cherished for years before reluctantly parting with it for the Dolomite.

We returned to the garage, and Doug ushered me into his office to review the paperwork. I found him to be very personable and friendly. He made us coffee and chatted easily about his work, informing me that he had been newly promoted to garage manager.

I told Doug I wanted the estate car for cash and carry work once I took over at the pet shop. He seemed genuinely interested in my plans and had a knack for seamlessly moving the conversation on to uncover details about my personal life. By the time I got up to leave, he knew I was divorced with a twelve-year-old son and seemed to empathise with my situation.

I mentioned wanting to part-exchange the Dolomite, so Doug arranged to come to my home and collect it the following day. I realised the Dolomite wasn't worth very much because of the rusting bodywork.

Once the transaction was completed, he stood up and shook my hand again. "I'll pop over to your house tomorrow and bring a trailer for the Dolomite," he said. "I'll make sure the Escort is given a full service, then I'll deliver it to you personally within the next few days," he promised, giving me another warm smile.

I walked to the bus stop with a new spring in my step. I suspected that Doug had designs on me. I would have to wait and see if my instincts were right.

The next day, Doug arrived, towing a trailer. His expert eye quickly assessed the Dolomite, and as expected, he wasn't impressed by the poor state of the rusty bodywork. I watched him skillfully winch the Dolomite onto the trailer and secure it.

Doug paused to admire the caravan standing to one side of my drive. "I don't think the Escort will be powerful enough to tow this caravan," he surmised after looking around it, noting the size of the caravan compared to the Escort's towing capacity.

I laughed. "Don't worry, I've no intention of trying to tow it. In fact, I've never plucked up the courage to attempt towing it since I got it."

"Well, if you should decide you want to take the caravan away, I've usually got one or two suitable cars equipped with tow bars that I would be happy for you to borrow," he offered, showing his trust in me.

I was surprised by his generosity. Although I doubted I would take him up on his offer, I appreciated his kindness.

Two days later, early in the evening, Doug arrived at my bungalow, driving my Escort estate. Byron and I rushed out, excited to see our new car parked on the driveway.

This was Byron's first time seeing it, and he seemed impressed, especially since the bodywork wasn't falling apart with rust like the Dolomite.

Doug suggested taking the car for a run down the motorway. I eagerly agreed to Doug's proposal, whereas Byron preferred staying home and watching his favourite program on the telly.

"I think you should drive the Escort," I told Doug. "I don't fancy driving on a motorway in a car I'm not yet accustomed to."

Doug was happy to drive. He took the wheel and didn't hold back, pushing the car to its limit in the fast lane. Despite his rough handling of the gears, the car's performance was impressive, offering a smooth ride.

We eventually reached the Little Chef, where Doug suggested a meal before our return journey.

We chatted easily over a casual meal of burgers and chips, followed by coffee. The conversation flowed as smoothly as the car's ride, making the journey back along the motorway seem shorter.

Doug eventually turned off the motorway at Northfleet and pulled up outside his office.

"I must lock up the garage now, but can I see you again - maybe take you out at the weekend?" Doug asked as I walked around to the driver's door of the Escort. I was pleased he had asked me out. I enjoyed his company, so I eagerly arranged for him to collect me on Saturday evening.

He waved me off, and I was finally alone in my new car for the first time, thrilled to be driving it home.

On Saturday, Byron was playing with his friends who lived near his nan and grandad's house, so he asked if he could stay there overnight. Meanwhile, I got ready for my date with Doug.

He arrived punctually and took me to a rural village pub for a quiet drink. The pub was a quaint little place with a cosy fireplace and old-fashioned decor, which added to the charm of the evening.

We chatted, getting to know each other better, and he kept me amused with his witty humour until closing time.

Back at my bungalow, I invited him in for a nightcap. To my surprise, he had brought his own, disappearing out to his car and returning with a bottle of whisky.

"I like to round off the evening with falling-down juice," he quipped. It was clearly his favourite tipple. He happily swigged it back while I stuck to my coffee, not sharing his enthusiasm for the strong stuff.

71

It soon became apparent that Doug was in no fit state to drive his car home. I offered him a bed for the night on my settee, which he gladly accepted.

Around midnight, he crashed out on the settee. I covered him with a blanket and left him in his drunken stupor while I retired to bed.

At two o'clock, I was rudely awakened by the doorbell ringing. I tumbled out of bed, still half asleep, and staggered to the door to see who was calling at such an unearthly hour.

I was shocked to find a tall, stern-looking policeman standing there. I could see his police car at the end of my drive with its lights flashing. I wondered what my neighbours would think if they happened to see it.

"Is that your car parked on the green outside your bungalow?" he asked. "I was driving past and noticed the driver's door wide open and no one in the car."

"Oh!" I gasped in surprise. "That's my friend's car. He must have forgotten to close the door."

"Anyone could have stolen the car as the keys are still inside it. I'll lock it up and bring you the keys," he said.

The policeman quickly returned and handed me the keys. His attitude had softened, and he smiled at me before turning to leave.

I thanked him, relieved that Doug's car hadn't been stolen. All the while, Doug hadn't stirred once from his alcohol-induced deep slumber.

Somewhat belatedly, it dawned on me that I had been standing in the lit doorway, scantily attired in a semi-transparent nightdress. I quickly closed the door, feeling both embarrassed and amused. No wonder the policeman had smiled!

Chapter Four

The Pet Shop

One evening the following week, my doorbell rang. I was amazed to find an attractive blonde girl visibly distressed on my doorstep. She burst into a flood of tears and eventually calmed down sufficiently to tell me what had happened.

Judging by her accent, I guessed she was an Aussie. "Your brother's girlfriend has just beaten me up," she sobbed.

I was stunned by her words. "What!" I gasped in disbelief. "She wouldn't do a thing like that. Are you absolutely certain it was her?"

The blonde girl pulled out a hankie and dabbed at her eyes. "Her name's Shelley, isn't it? I was in your local pub just down the road with a friend having a quiet drink. When I went to the Ladies, Shelley and two other girls followed me there. She accused me of seeing Roger behind her back. Then she started hitting me. She threatened me, warning me to keep away from him."

The thought of Shelley becoming an aggressive figure in a pub toilet was beyond my comprehension. Her words left me utterly gobsmacked. Yet, this Aussie girl was adamant that it had happened. If her story was really true, it revealed a side of Shelley that had been concealed until now, which stirred my curiosity.

What was my brother thinking, betraying Shelley when they were about to start a life together? I was utterly baffled; I couldn't reconcile this behaviour with the brother I knew.

"So, you've been going out with my brother?" I asked, trying to keep my tone neutral.

The girl nodded. "Naturally, he didn't mention anything about Shelley. He drove past your place one evening and pointed it out to me. That's how I knew where you lived."

I felt at a loss as to how I could help this girl. Roger and Shelley had been together for a good few years, so I couldn't understand what possessed my brother to be unfaithful to Shelley.

As this girl was a stranger to me, I hesitated to invite her indoors. Her story might have a different angle, one that Shelley had uncovered. It was conceivable that this Aussie girl was attempting to lure Roger away from Shelley, and Shelley had caught wind of it.

By now, the girl had regained her composure. The anger in her eyes was unmistakable.

"You can relay a message to Shelley when you see her saying that she's welcome to Roger and tell your brother he can go to hell!"

She turned and stomped off up the drive. I closed the door, still reeling from the bizarre encounter. None of it made sense, but I was determined to confront my brother and unravel this mystery.

By the end of November, Roger and Shelley had moved into their house, so I called in to see how they were adapting to their new life.

I found Roger at home alone as Shelley was enjoying an evening out with her mates. This gave me the opportunity to ask him about the mysterious Aussie girl.

When I recounted her unexpected appearance on my doorstep, he looked stunned, then merely shrugged, laughing it off. He dismissed it as a momentary lapse on his part.

Nevertheless, he was visibly taken aback that Shelley had found out. "It just shows how much she cares about me, making a scene in a pub toilet," he boasted, sounding chuffed. "She hasn't mentioned my little indiscretion to me."

"I never imagined that you would two-time Shelley," I said, surprised by his casual admission. "Obviously, I don't know you as well as I thought."

Roger quickly changed the subject and gave me a brief tour of the two-up, two-down, end-of-terrace house. The small lobby by the front door led into a good-sized kitchen.

"My first job will be to replace these old units because Shelley wants a more modern kitchen," he said and then led me into the adjoining lounge, which was once the original shop, now transformed into a cosy living space.

"You've made it very comfortable in here," I remarked, admiring the three-piece suite.

"Shelley's parents gave us that suite as a house-warming present. The shag pile carpet looks past its best, but I've arranged for it to be professionally cleaned, which I'm hoping will give it a new lease of life."

As I was leaving, Roger invited Byron and me to join him and Shelley on Christmas Day. "It'll be our first attempt at preparing a Christmas dinner, so you will come, won't you?"

I grinned. "It sounds like you want Byron and me to be guinea pigs for your dubious cooking skills! Of course, we'd love to come."

At the beginning of December, I received an excited phone call from Joan. "We're in! We moved into the flat above the supermarket about a week ago and haven't stopped working. We've been so busy getting unpacked and sorted out. The shop is really hectic - I'm so glad we've got some dependable staff to help us settle in. At the moment, we are simply continuing along the same lines as the previous owners. Cyril still has plans for changes to the deli and the off-licence. We've already got a pleasant young couple as tenants for the second flat, which is really handy."

"It must be quite a change of lifestyle for you after living in that large house at Reepham," I remarked.

"The area does seem a little rough. It's mainly a council estate with blocks of flats that have seen better days. Cyril worries about shoplifting, so he hovers near the door, watching everyone closely as they leave."

I laughed. "I bet your customers won't take very kindly to him scrutinising them suspiciously."

"Oh, I'm sure he'll calm down once he's got the close-circuit TV installed that he's ordered."

Joan's words didn't reassure me much. I still felt they were taking on too much at their time of life.

"Stella has had the results of the tests from the hospital," Joan informed me. "Unfortunately, they have confirmed that she has blocked fallopian tubes, making her unable to conceive."

"Oh, poor Stella. Is she very upset?"

"She's coming to terms with it, but all is not lost. They have given her the option of trying for a test tube baby instead. Stella is keen to give it a go, but it will cost a lot of money. It's just as well they are earning good money in Saudi!"

Joan enquired about the progress of my purchase of the pet shop. I told her that it would probably be finalised after Christmas.

"Oh, and, like you, I've also got an estate car ready for doing the cash and carry work. It's in much better condition than my rusty old Dolomite."

December 1983 saw several landmark news stories that would go down in history. On the 6th, the very first heart and lung transplant in the United Kingdom was performed at Harefield Hospital.

On December 8th, the House of Lords voted to allow the broadcasting of its proceedings, offering an interesting viewpoint via television.

Sadly, on the 17th, the IRA caused disruption and suffering when they exploded a car bomb outside Harrods, killing six people – three policemen and three pedestrians. An additional ninety people were injured.

At home, I finally received the exciting news I'd been waiting for. I would take over the pet shop at the beginning of January. I had a new year and a new vocation to look forward to.

Christmas arrived, but not without another IRA attack. This time, the bomb exploded in Oxford Street, a place I knew well, but fortunately, no one was injured. However, the news of the attack cast a shadow over the festive season, reminding me of the uncertainty and fear that had become a part of our lives.

I didn't see much of Doug over Christmas, as he spent it with his family. Byron was over the moon to receive his very own Atari computer. Still, he had to wait patiently until Boxing Day before he could enjoy playing Breakout and Asteroids.

We spent Christmas Day at Roger and Shelley's house, joining them for a delicious dinner. Shelley's first attempt at preparing and cooking a Christmas dinner was a resounding success. As we chatted during our meal, the radio entertained us in the background, airing the Christmas number one song - the oldie, 'Only You', newly released by The Flying Pickets.

Afterwards, we relaxed with freshly brewed coffee and treats, watching television. The main feature film on ITV was Superman. We didn't fancy that, so we watched the comedy film 'Life of Brian' by the Monty Python team instead.

On Saturday, January 7th, Anne closed the pet shop early as it was her last day. I joined her and Linda to help conduct a complete inventory of the stock.

After the long and laborious task of counting everything, we finally completed the stocktaking, marking the end of Anne's tenure and the beginning of a new phase when the shop would come under my management the following Monday.

As I prepared for my first day at the shop, I saw Byron off to school before driving to Sidcup. Over breakfast, I warned Byron that if the shop didn't work out, we would have no alternative other than to sell up and move.

"But the shop will work out," Byron insisted. "There's no reason why it won't."

I hoped he was right and tried to think positively as I parked in the small rear yard behind the shop. I noticed Linda's motorbike was already there.

I walked down the passageway past the piles of straw, hay, and sawdust, feeling a little nervous. This was a significant new step in my life, and I was unsure what to expect. But I was also filled with anticipation and excitement about what surprises and challenges awaited me. The thought of being my own boss and the potential for the shop to become a more prosperous business filled me with a sense of adventure.

Linda had opened the shop and hung large bunches of bird feeders outside. She greeted me warmly and immediately offered to make some tea. Her gesture instantly made me feel welcome. With no customers in the shop, I followed her into the storeroom and tidied my desk.

"Anne has let quite a few things go out of stock, so I'll go through the catalogue, showing you which items need to be ordered," Linda suggested as she came over and handed me a mug of tea.

Just then, the doorbell jangled, so Linda hurried out to the shop. I gazed around the dingy, cobwebby room with its solitary, inadequate, bare light bulb hardly penetrating the gloom. This was the room I had envisaged being divided so that half of the space could be converted into a room to house the tropical fish. Despite its current state, I saw the potential for transformation. I felt hopeful that my dream could become a reality with some renovations.

A slight movement on the wall beside my desk caught my attention. I looked up and, to my utter horror, saw a large black cockroach leisurely creeping up the wall. I shuddered, giving an involuntary scream, and then hastily fled into the shop, still reeling from the repulsive sight.

Linda had just finished serving a customer. She turned to me, looking concerned. She had heard my scream.

"I've just seen a cockroach crawling up the wall," I said, taking a swig of tea to calm my nerves. "We don't have cockroaches, do we? Anne never mentioned them."

Linda laughed. "Oh, yes, don't worry about them. They won't bother you. They're not really a problem."

Linda's words didn't help to calm my nerves. I detested creepy crawlies; in fact, I had a deep-seated phobia about them. Since childhood, I had been petrified of insects, especially the ones that scuttled and crawled.

During the year I lived on a converted barge on the River Medway when Byron was a baby, I was horrified to discover grottles that looked like enormous woodlice emerging from the bilge and scuttling around. The sight of the cockroach resurrected those awful memories and sent shivers down my spine. I couldn't shake off the feeling of unease.

"Oh, and I don't suppose Anne mentioned Pete, the ghost, either?" Linda asked with a mischievous glint in her eye, clearly enjoying seeing me look mystified.

The news of a ghost residing in the shop didn't surprise me. I could easily imagine the gloomy storeroom being haunted. "How do you know his name is Pete?" I asked.

"Well, Anne named him Pete after the bags of peat we sell. If you find something goes missing and then later it turns up in an unexpected place, it's probably Pete messing about. It's just his humorous way of letting you know he's around."

"I don't mind that, so long as he doesn't suddenly materialise," I said.

The shop started to get busy, so we turned our attention to serving customers. Linda helped me if I couldn't find what a customer wanted.

Some of the regular customers popped in for a chat along with their purchases. Linda introduced me to them, and I noticed she was particularly good at remembering their names and their pets' names, which always brought a smile to their faces.

Once the shop was quiet again, Linda guided me through drawing up my first order for the wholesaler, Wundapets, who delivered once a week. I was surprised by the sheer volume of stock needed, but I was determined to learn the intricacies of the business.

"Anne didn't bother re-ordering many items because she knew she was leaving. She left it for you to decide which lines you'd like to stock," Linda explained.

"Well, until I find my feet, we'll just restock with the best-selling lines and essentials." I appreciated Linda's knowledge and expertise with the re-ordering. She suggested items I had never heard of but she insisted they were vital.

I had to muster the courage to use the phone on my desk to place the order. Glancing up nervously at the walls, I searched for more cockroaches while I spoke on the phone, unable to shake off the jittery feeling. The thought of these creepy crawlies scurrying around while I worked was enough to make my skin crawl. I would not be spending much time at my desk.

As I was about to leave the storeroom, I paused to check the contents of some boxes stacked on the shelves.

My nerves jangled as I caught sight of an enormous spider sitting in its web in the corner above the sink, its hairy legs sprawled in all directions. The sight made me shudder with revulsion.

'This place is fast becoming my worst nightmare,' I thought and hurried into the bright shop. Linda was busy arranging the window display. "Do you know there's a huge spider in the storeroom?" I asked, trying to keep my voice steady.

"Do you mean the one in the corner, above the sink? He's been living there for ages," Linda said offhandedly. The spider obviously didn't bother her, which left me puzzled.

"If he stays, then you will be solely responsible for making drinks and washing up," I stipulated. "I'm not going anywhere near the sink with that hideous thing dangling above me."

The only source of heat in the shop was a portable Calor gas heater standing behind the counter, which struggled and failed to keep the whole shop warm, especially during the chilly winter days. Linda tended to monopolise it, sitting on top of it to stay warm between serving customers. Her jeans were so tight that they weren't in any danger of catching fire.

Linda also wore killer high heels all day. How she managed to ride her motorbike while wearing them was a mystery to me.

I noticed that Anne hadn't bothered with overalls. I felt a matching pair of overalls for Linda and me would make us look smarter and more efficient. I suggested it to Linda, and she thought it was a great idea.

"An overall will help to keep my clothes clean. It's surprising how grubby you can get, humping bags of coal, corn or peanuts around," she remarked.

"In that case, I'll buy a couple next time I'm in town." I glanced at the bags of coal stacked near the shop door in the gardening section. "Do you sell much coal?"

"This time of year, we do, but not for the rest of the year. I think it's more trouble than it's worth."

"In that case, once Spring arrives, I shan't order any more," I said emphatically. "Somehow, selling coal doesn't fit in with the pet trade."

At lunchtime, Linda suggested some delicious bacon butties, freshly made at the cafe, two shops along on the parade. It was run by a friendly Italian family who dispatched their teenage daughter to deliver our sandwiches.

Linda and I chatted, getting to know each other better between eating our sandwiches and serving the occasional customer. Linda told me about her family. She lived a few streets away with her widowed mum and two brothers. Jason, her younger brother, was still at school. Her older brother, a huge Michael Jackson fan, had even taken the trouble to have his name changed by deed poll to Michael Jackson.

Linda also told me about her boyfriend, Vick. She admitted that he was older than her, married, and living at Erith. However, Vick and his wife had no children. He worked as a D.J., playing music at gigs most evenings. Linda often accompanied him to help out.

She also made the startling confession that she claimed unemployment benefit while being paid cash for her work in the shop at the end of each week.

I realised Linda didn't earn much of a wage. Nevertheless, I was a little shocked by her confession, but I decided to ignore her illegal activity.

"I shall pretend you never told me that. If you get caught, it will be your problem to deal with," I warned her.

Linda quickly changed the subject and told me about her unshakable ambition to step into the world of modelling. Her tall, willowy figure and attractive face certainly did fit the bill. She spoke passionately about her dream, her eyes lighting up with excitement as she described her plans to have professional photos taken for her portfolio and visit some agencies, hoping to be accepted onto their books.

I could only admire her courage and wish her good luck in pursuing this highly competitive profession.

During the afternoon, a man entered the shop wearing tight jeans, a black leather jacket, and sporting an earring. This was Vick, Linda's enigmatic boyfriend.

He greeted us with a barely audible 'hello' and remained mostly silent, his expression inscrutable. Yet, Linda seemed able to decipher his every emotion as I struggled to interpret his indeterminate face.

Vick stayed for a coffee and then left after arranging to meet Linda that evening.

Linda had her own key to the shop, allowing her to come in on Sundays to feed the birds and animals as she lived locally. It was a convenient arrangement, but I soon discovered the reason for her eagerness.

On Tuesday morning, I arrived at the shop and was surprised to find dog beds scattered on the floor in the storeroom. They hadn't been there on Monday when I closed the shop.

I realised that Linda had been taking advantage of the closed shop at night to bring Vick back after an evening at a gig for some quiet time together, as they had nowhere else to go for their private canoodling.

Despite my disapproval of Linda's liberties, I realised she had a crucial role in the shop's operations. I depended on her to open the shop each morning and to care for the animals on Sundays. So, with no apparent damage done, I chose to remain silent instead of reprimanding her.

As I entered the shop, I was greeted by an unexpected scene. Pedro was perched on the shelf containing the jars of various birdseeds. He was obviously in a mischievous mood because he was busy ripping the labels off the jars and spitting them into the bins below, where the dog biscuits and hamster food were stored.

I plucked up the courage to coax him onto the back of my hand as I had seen Linda do and return him to his cage, where he protested loudly.

Linda was out in the back room, feeding the animals. I called her to come and replace the torn and missing labels.

She laughed when she saw what Pedro had done.

"I think he does that to get attention," she said. "Or when something has upset him. I'm always having to redo the labels on those jars."

Tuesday was the day for the meat man's delivery. The horse meat, resembling large joints of lean beef had to be cut into smaller pieces. The bulk bags of mince needed to be weighed and wrapped, as did the green tripe that stunk something awful. I was thankful once it was all cut up and bagged, ready to be stowed away in the large chest freezer that stood against the wall behind the counter.

Linda warned me not to sell the white mice to anyone who wanted to buy them in bulk, as they would undoubtedly become food for their pet reptiles.

She also explained that the scales on the garden centre side of the shop were solely for weighing slug pellets and fertiliser.

"Whatever you do, never weigh slug pellets in the pet shop scales because they're poisonous to animals." Linda's warning emphasised the importance of understanding the products we handled. Since the shop was divided by the large central shelving unit, I felt confident that such a mistake was unlikely to occur.

On Wednesday, the hay man arrived to restock the bags of straw, hay, and sawdust stacked on the floor in the rear passage.

Anne called in at the shop on Thursday to see how I was coping. She brought two enormous St Bernard dogs, part of her breeding program. They were beautiful dogs, but I wasn't keen on all their drooling. Anne kept a towel handy to mop up their saliva.

After Anne had left, a lady came in with a little black Scottie dog. "Watch that dog," Linda whispered to me. "It always cocks its leg against a bag of corn." Linda served the lady, and sure enough, as she turned to leave, the Scottie dog paused to cock his leg.

Linda sighed. "You see – every time! I'll get the mop and clean the floor."

A man wanted a dog identity disc engraved. Linda was busy, so I decided to have a go. The engraving tool was kept on the bench in the storeroom. My first attempt at engraving was abysmal. The scratchy marks were practically illegible. I tried a second disc, but that also ended in dismal failure. Linda came to see how I was managing.

"It's no use, Linda, I can't get the hang of this engraving. My writing just isn't neat enough. I shall have to delegate this job to you," I said, frustrated by my hopeless efforts.

Linda smiled. "I don't mind - let me have a go." She took a fresh disc from a box and neatly engraved it.

"You make it look easy," I remarked.

"I've had plenty of practise," Linda said dismissively. She handed me the engraved disc, and I hurried back to the customer, who, by now, was getting a little impatient at the protracted wait he had endured for his disc.

The best-selling items at this time of year were undoubtedly the wild birdseed and the peanuts. We sold the peanuts loose by the pound and also in red string bags. By Friday, they were running low, so I decided to drive to the cash and carry warehouse at Erith, leaving Linda in charge at the shop.

I found the warehouse quite easily and spent some time browsing around the aisles, collecting various things that caught my eye. I needed help to lift the large sack of peanuts, weighing over fifty pounds, into the back of my estate car.

Back at the shop, I managed to lug the sack through the passageway and into the shop. Linda saw me struggling and rushed over to give me a hand.

Despite her slim build, Linda obviously had strong arms as she heaved the sack into position beside the sacks of corn and feed. I realised I was far from being at the peak of my fitness, as I had to stop and catch my breath after the exertion.

"I'm sure doing more cash and carrying will toughen me up," I gasped.

"It'll kill or cure," Linda quipped with a grin. "I'll go and make a recuperative cup of tea."

Friday afternoon, a man called in and introduced himself as Geoff. "I own Geoff's Cages – the small shop in the High Street. I make and sell animal cages. I always supplied Anne with her cages, so I hope I can continue to supply you, too."

The rabbit and guinea pig cages we stocked in the shop looked sturdy and well-built. I assured him his cages were a valuable addition to our stock, and he could definitely continue supplying them. He beamed and shook my hand, pleased with our business arrangement.

Friday evening, just before closing time, the lady living in the upstairs flat came into the shop to pay her rent. She was an attractive young woman with shoulder-length blonde hair and introduced herself with a friendly smile. She explained that she called in at the shop every Friday.

"Friday is my payday, so you'll get your rent without fail," she promised. I signed her rent book and noted that the payments in the book were made regularly every Friday, just as she had said.

Saturday was our busiest day, with a queue of customers stretching down the shop as far as the door. The shop was abuzz with activity and noise, from the sound of the cash register to the chatter of customers trying to be heard above the cacophony from all the birds.

Two young boys wanted a goldfish each, so I took them to the separate area in the wide passageway where they could choose their fish from the assortment swimming around in the large tank. They selected two with distinctive markings, but they proved elusive to catch. I chased them with a net until I finally caught them and transferred them to a plastic bag half filled with water, which I carefully sealed. Meanwhile, the queue in the shop was getting longer, and some customers were getting restless.

At least keeping busy all day meant the time passed quickly, and the takings were more than double those on a weekday. At the end of the day, I could afford to pay Linda and myself our wages.

I couldn't bear the thought of Pedro being alone in his cage on Sunday when the shop was closed, so, feeling responsible for him, I decided to take him home.

Byron was intrigued by Pedro. Although he hadn't met him before, he quickly got him talking, even managing to elicit his infectious belly laugh.

However, Pedro proved to be quite a handful when I let him loose in the lounge. He immediately flew up on top of the open door and started tearing strips of wallpaper off the wall. After shooing him off the door, he landed on the carpet and began strutting around, screeching loudly.

Then he spotted a curious Jojo peering at him from the doorway. Pedro fearlessly rushed at Jojo, who wisely dashed into the kitchen and escaped through the cat flap. Meanwhile, Tia was curled up, asleep on my bed, utterly oblivious to the chaos.

I managed to coax Pedro back into his cage, but he soon caused a commotion when I switched on the television. He protested with deafening screeches and chatter that drowned out the television. I had no option but to cover his cage to quiet him down.

On Sunday afternoon, I rang Joan for a chat to tell her about my first week at the shop and to hear her news on how they were coping with their supermarket.

When I spoke to Joan, I was concerned to hear the exhaustion in her voice. She had spent all morning mopping the floor in the shop while it was closed, filling shelves, and tidying up ready for Monday morning.

"Cyril has been making batches of bread pudding for the deli, using his special recipe, and it's proved to be a great success. No sooner is the bread pudding put out on the counter than it's snapped up and sold out!"

"I'm not surprised. Cyril gave me his recipe, and it's the best bread pudding I've ever tasted," I said. "Any news from Stella and Mick yet?"

"I spoke to Stella last week. They will be coming home soon to begin trying for a test tube baby. She's really excited about it. We're all keeping our fingers crossed, hoping it will work."

"Tell Stella I'm rooting for her the next time you speak to her."

Monday morning, I returned Pedro to the shop. I arrived to find it closed, as Linda was late, so the shop hadn't opened on time. She arrived looking pale.

"I've had one of my migraines – I get them quite often," she said. "But I took some tablets, and I'm fine now," she assured me.

"You do look a little washed out," I observed. "Are you sure you're fit to work today?"

"I'm all right now – really I am," Linda insisted. "I'll make us some tea, and then I'll be fighting fit!"

We had just finished hanging up the bird feeders and standing goods outside on the pavement when Wundapet's lorry drew up. They had arrived with my first delivery, which was a large order. Linda and I were busy filling up the shelves with the new stock. I had a range of cat baskets, but being bulky, I couldn't find a home for them.

"Linda, do you have any ideas where to put these baskets?"

Linda glanced around and pointed to a narrow shelf along the front of the shop above the door, which I hadn't noticed before. "I think that shelf is just wide enough, and they would look great lined up along there," she suggested.

As Linda meticulously arranged the cat baskets using a step ladder, I took a moment to admire the fully stocked shelves. The sight filled me with a deep sense of satisfaction, knowing that we had worked hard to make the shop look its best.

Linda and I were now dressed in matching overalls, which gave us a more professional appearance when serving the customers.

Once the word got out that Flights had a new owner, the reps started pouring in, each eager to sell their brand of pet supplies or gardening requisites. I listened patiently to their sales pitch but usually made it clear that I wasn't interested in their offerings.

"You tease those poor reps and lead them on by looking as if you're really keen on what they're trying to sell you," Linda chided.

I grinned. "I don't intend to be rude to them, but the reps come in here uninvited, so they shouldn't be surprised if I don't make a purchase."

My learning curve at the shop was steep, and Linda's guidance was instrumental. She stressed the importance of checking the fish tanks each morning and removing any dead fish. "Just feed them to the grass snake in the vivarium," she advised. "They make a tasty snack for him."

I wasn't very keen on having a grass snake in the shop, even though it wasn't much trouble to look after. Then, one day, it disappeared. I arrived at the shop one morning and found Linda in a panic.

"The grass snake has escaped," she informed me, her voice tinged with disbelief. "I've hunted everywhere, but there's no sign of it."

I looked around uneasily, half expecting to see it slithering out from some nook or cranny. "Go and check the storeroom and back room while I search around in here," I told her.

I checked the rabbit and guinea pig hutches in case it had crept inside. The animals all looked contented, and their cages showed no sign of being invaded.

I was down on my hands and knees, peering beneath the central shelving unit, when a man entered the shop. He looked at me with surprise and amusement as I grovelled on the floor.

"Have you lost something?" he asked, trying to stifle a chuckle.

"Er, yes, I have," I admitted, hastily standing up and brushing myself down.

"It wouldn't happen to be a snake, would it?" the man continued with a wry smile.

I gasped with surprise. "Have you found one?"

"I own the chemist's shop opposite. I unlocked the shop this morning and discovered, to my amazement, a snake curled up asleep on my doormat. I realised it must have crawled through my letter box as it's low on the front door. I deduced that the snake most probably came from your shop."

Linda appeared from the storeroom, so I told her to take the vivarium across the road and collect the snake.

"Imagine the snake crossing a busy road safely," she said, sounding bemused.

"Somehow, it escaped from the vivarium, squeezed out through our letter box and then slithered across the road to the chemist's shop," I said. "It probably escaped during the night when the road was quiet."

"Perhaps it had a headache and wanted some aspirin," Linda joked with a laugh. She accompanied the man to his shop to retrieve the intrepid grass snake.

I decided the shop could do without grass snakes on its shelves, so I had no intention of replacing it once it was sold.

Linda was tidying one of the window displays the next day when she called out, "Here comes Clive – he's one of our regulars."

I watched through the window as a three-wheeled disability car was fearlessly parked outside the shop on the double yellow line by the bus stop. A man climbed out with difficulty and struggled across the pavement using two sticks.

Linda opened the door for him, and he soon made himself comfortable on the chair beside the counter. He bought some dog treats and chatted for a while. Then he produced some photos to show us of his little dog. We weren't too busy, so Linda offered him a mug of tea.

After Clive had departed, Linda explained that he lived alone with his little dog. "I think he gets lonely and enjoys calling in here for a chat. I hope you didn't mind me making him some tea."

"No, of course, I didn't mind. We should always try to make our customers feel welcome, even the ones who allow their dogs to cock their legs on our merchandise!"

Roger and Shelley called in to see me one evening to find out how I was coping with running the pet shop. We chatted over coffee in the lounge, and I told them about the fiasco with the grass snake and the problems Pedro caused when I brought him home.

"You need a large notice in the window proclaiming that the shop is under new management," Shelley declared. "I've got a day off from work tomorrow. How about I come to the shop and give you a hand setting up a new window display?"

I brightened up at her suggestion. "I think that's an excellent idea. A new window display will emphasise that the shop has a new owner."

True to her word, Shelley arrived at the shop the following morning in her flashy red TR7 sports car. She was bursting with enthusiasm and energy – just what I

91

needed. She brought a large banner she had made to stick on the window, announcing: 'Under New Management'.

Shelley thoroughly enjoyed setting up the new display, which included aquariums, fish accessories, and the usual bird and pet requisites. Linda and I were very impressed with the finished display, catching the eye of passers-by.

Shelley then energetically set about cleaning and tidying all the shelves. However, she refused to go anywhere near the spider's web in the storeroom, so the spider remained undisturbed.

The shop now looked more vibrant and inviting, all thanks to Shelley's creative touch. I appreciated her help and offered to pay her, but she refused, adamant that it was done as a favour.

She told me that she and Roger planned to take a break and go to the coast for a few days over the weekend. "You can make use of my car while we're away if you like," she offered.

The thought of driving around in a flashy sports car was exhilarating, so I readily accepted her generous offer.

"Roger and I will drop it off at your place before we head for the coast," Shelley said as she was leaving.

Friday evening, Roger and Shelley arrived at my bungalow in separate cars. Shelley parked her TR7 on my drive and then joined Roger in his car. "I'll collect it next week," Shelley called out as I waved them off.

Half an hour later, Doug turned up and was eager to take the sports car for a spin. We drove down the motorway once again to the Little Chef, stopping there for a snack before coming home. We each took turns driving the TR7. Doug, being interested in cars, was really excited to drive it.

On Saturday, I enjoyed driving the sports car to the shop and home again that evening with Pedro in his cage on the passenger seat next to me. He squawked noisily, adding his own commentary to the journey.

I drove to my parents' house Sunday morning and offered to take Dad in the sports car to visit his sister, my Auntie Rene. She and Uncle Harold had recently moved from their Edwardian semi to a small self-contained flat in an old people's complex in a village outside Dartford.

Their ground-floor flat was close to the main entrance. Auntie Rene spotted us arriving and waved excitedly through her window.

I offered to make some tea in her small kitchenette and then brought a tray of tea and biscuits through to the compact lounge/dining room. Uncle Harold didn't say much, as usual; he just carried on reading his newspaper while we chatted. Auntie Rene wanted to know all about the shop and then asked after Tia.

"I've got her booked into her next show," I informed my aunt. "It's being held at Maidstone in March. Tia did so well at her first show last August; I hope she'll do as well this time."

Auntie Rene seemed very happy in her new flat. "There's a communal hall where we can have a meal if we don't feel like cooking. They run bingo sessions and whist drives there every week, so Harold and I often go along to play a game in the evening."

"You were lucky this flat became available. It seems ideal for you," Dad said, pleased that his sister had settled in so well. She had spent most of her adult life living in the Edwardian semi-detached house a few streets from the Crescent.

"It's been quite a lifestyle change for us, but it's definitely for the better now that we're getting on in years," my aunt affirmed, accepting the changes life brings with age.

On our way home, Dad wanted to pick up a large bag of potatoes. Having given up driving some time ago, he was eager to make use of the car. He had spotted an advertisement for potatoes at a farm shop in the countryside along our route.

We arrived at the shop and struggled to fit the bulky bag of potatoes into the compact sports car but finally managed it. Then, we continued on our journey home along the scenic country lanes.

Because Dad suffered from emphasaemia, he wound down his window to feel the cool wind on his face, making it easier for him to breathe. The sports car ride was a source of pure enjoyment for him. I could tell he longed to have the roof down, giving him all the fresh air he could want, but the chilly February weather made it impractical.

Chapter Five

Animals Run Amok

Byron wanted to earn extra pocket money, so I offered him a Saturday job cleaning the animal cages at the shop. He wasn't overly keen on the work but had to knuckle down and get on with it as he wanted the money.

Saturday morning, while the shop was at its busiest, he cleaned the cages and hutches in the back room. Then, Saturday afternoon, he cleaned the cages in the shop.

Linda would make us all coffee mid-morning, which made a welcome break for Byron. He liked Linda, and they quickly developed a rapport.

One Saturday morning, as we were busy serving customers, I noticed Byron's coffee left untouched on the counter, getting cold. He was in the back room, engrossed in cleaning the cages, seemingly oblivious that Linda had called him to come for his coffee break.

I called out to him and continued serving several more customers while Linda served in the gardening section. Still, there was no sign of Byron. Once Linda was free, I asked her to go and fetch him.

She disappeared through the walkway past the fish tanks but quickly returned a few minutes later, bursting with laughter.

"You've got to come and see this," she chuckled, beckoning me.

I hurried after her through the storeroom and into the back room. There, I found Byron stuck in a tricky situation. He was crouching beneath a bench full of cages, nursing a fire extinguisher, his thumb pressed hard on the end of the nozzle to prevent it from exploding in a sea of foam.

"What on earth are you doing?" I exclaimed. Byron just looked sheepish.

"He was meddling with that fire extinguisher," Linda said, sounding amused. "It's one that's kept under the bench. He's accidentally knocked the cap off that keeps the nozzle sealed up, and now he doesn't dare move a muscle!"

"I've been stuck here for ages," Byron complained. "I did call out, but you didn't hear me. If I try to move this fire extinguisher will go off."

I couldn't help laughing at his predicament. "How are we going to rescue you? Any ideas, Linda?"

She hesitated, glancing around. "I'll open that door leading into the passage and the back door into the yard. Then I'll try to replace Byron's thumb with my thumb and take the extinguisher outside, where the foam won't do any harm."

Linda's plan sounded feasible, but implementing it was far from easy. Once the doors were opened, giving access to the backyard, Linda crouched beside Byron. She managed to get her thumb on the end of the nozzle, with only a minimal amount of foam escaping. She struggled to her feet, hugging the extinguisher, and then dashed outside with it.

She soon returned, minus the extinguisher, chuckling at what she had done. "I've tossed it over the wall into the hardware shop's yard," she confessed. "The foam went everywhere."

"What!" I gasped in dismay. "You shouldn't have done that. The owner of the corner shop will be furious when he discovers his yard covered in foam."

"Oh, I don't think he'll mind," Linda said. "Besides, he's not the owner; he only manages the shop. The owner also owns the tool hire shop, further along on the parade."

Byron stood up and stretched, looking visibly relieved and a little embarrassed. He had become stiff and cramped under the bench. "I thought I was never going to be rescued!" he exclaimed.

"If you ask Linda nicely, I'm sure she'll make you a fresh mug of coffee," I said, feeling a little sorry for him. "I expect you could do with a hot drink after your ordeal."

Saturday afternoon, while the shop was fairly quiet, we had a visit from Linda's mum and younger brother. Her mum came in laden with shopping bags, looking weary. She slumped onto the chair beside the counter, dropping her shopping bags on the floor.

Linda introduced me to her mum and brother, Jason, who seemed a quiet lad. Now, in his final year at school, he bore a striking resemblance to his sister. The shop made a convenient place for them to stop off for a rest on their journey home.

Linda went to the storeroom to make tea because her mum said she was gasping for a cuppa. She spoke with a slight speech impediment. When she asked Linda to bring her some sugar, she pronounced it 'hoo-ha', but Linda understood exactly what her mum meant.

I soon discovered Linda's mum made this stop for tea a regular occurrence whenever she was walking home from the shops. She appeared unaware that if the shop became busy with a queue of customers, she might be in the way with her shopping bags cluttering up the floor.

I was reluctant to complain to Linda that her mum was taking advantage. I realised that Anne must have been OK with Linda's mum coming in regularly. Linda's mum obviously assumed nothing had changed now that I was in charge.

I could tell that Linda and her mum were quite close. Linda was always willing to accommodate her mum's needs, even if it meant disrupting the shop's routine. I decided it was best to leave things as they were and say nothing, as I didn't want to fall out with Linda.

A little later, after Linda's mum and brother had left, a friend of Linda's came in, hoping for a coffee and a chat. Linda introduced me to Terry, another biker dressed in a black leather jacket and jeans with his crash helmet tucked under his arm. Despite his rocker appearance with long sideburns, Terry was quite charming, regaling us with stories about his work with the local council, painting houses.

I was surprised Linda didn't prefer Terry as a boyfriend to Vick, who was older and married, but her affair with Vick was none of my business. I knew they had been together for a long time, and Linda seemed content with their relationship.

After Terry had gone, we continued to serve a steady stream of customers. The lady with the Scottie dog came in, and this time the dog cocked his leg against the bag of peanuts.

A man entered and waited in the queue to be served. He became impatient and decided to liven things up by calling to Linda: "Do you have anything to cure my dog's wind?" His unexpected request made the other customers smile and chuckle.

Linda grinned. "You should try a cork!" She quipped. The man laughed, appreciating the joke. The other customers couldn't help laughing at her remark, lightening the mood in the shop.

"Linda, that's not the way to keep our customers happy," I chided.

She merely shrugged. "Don't worry, I'm sure we stock something more suitable to cure his dog's flatulence."

Saturday evenings, after a busy day in the shop, I felt too tired to go home and cook a meal. Instead, Byron and I usually opted for a takeaway.

Further along the parade, an Indian restaurant prepared really excellent food. I would ring them with an order and then collect it after I had locked up the shop. Some Saturdays, for a change, we would opt for a Chinese or fish and chips from takeaways nearer to home or a Kentucky fried meal picked up in Dartford. We looked forward to these Saturday evening treats after an exhausting day in the shop.

March arrived, but spring was yet to grace us with its warmth. However, the season's charm was evident in the blooming spring plants we now had for sale, along with various bulbs. Each morning, we would carefully arrange them outside the shop on a bench, adding a vibrant touch of spring to the chilly weather.

An elderly lady came into the shop and asked if I would be interested in buying the baby budgerigars she bred. She explained that she had previously supplied them to Anne. I arranged to visit her home on Sunday when the shop was closed to see what birds she had available.

I drove over to her house at Sidcup on Sunday morning, and she showed me her well-kept aviary in the back garden. The budgerigars were chirping noisily, and they all looked contented and healthy. She even had a couple of rare white albino budgies, but these weren't available for sale. She pointed out the pretty blue and green baby budgies. We agreed on a price, and I arranged for her to bring them to the shop the following week.

As I drove home, I felt pleased with the deal I had struck. Despite the changing times, budgies continued to be a very popular pet.

The following Saturday was the day of Tia's second show at the Maidstone and Medway Cat Show, which was being held at Maidstone. This would be her first show entered in the adult section, where she could win a challenge certificate if she came first in her open class. Three challenge certificates must be won at three separate shows under three different judges for a cat to be made up to a champion. I was hopeful that Tia might be awarded her first certificate.

I would be leaving Linda to cope alone in the shop, not that she minded. She suggested bringing her brother along to help, which I agreed was a good idea.

I discovered a large sign advertising Flights tucked away in the storeroom, so I decided to book a stall at the cat show. I could then display the sign and sell an assortment of cat accessories from the shop.

At home, I had been preparing Tia's coat for the show, carefully grooming and brushing her to ensure she looked her best.

However, Tia was more interested in playing chasing games with Jojo in the back garden. She was only allowed her freedom outside when I could keep an eye on her. I watched with amusement through the patio doors as mischievous Tia enticed Jojo to the top of the Bramley apple tree, then nimbly leapt down, leaving poor Jojo stranded, desperately trying to hang on to the topmost branch. It took him a while to work out how to reverse back down the tree.

Roger and Shelley offered to help me and Byron run the stall on Saturday, which pleased me immensely. On Friday evening, Roger took me to the shop in his work van. We loaded it up with everything a feline could possibly need: cat baskets, bedding, litter, food, supplements, accessories, toys, and treats.

Early Saturday morning, I drove to Maidstone with Byron. Tia, looking very fluffy, was tucked up safely in her basket. Roger and Shelley followed us in Roger's van.

The weather let us down with heavy rain, making driving difficult. The rain refused to let up all day, but we made the most of the occasion, regardless.

At the hall, I left Roger, Shelley and Byron setting up the stall. The board advertising Flights was prominently displayed on the wall behind the stall.

Meanwhile, I nervously took Tia through the vetting-in procedure. Then I settled her in her pen with the compulsory all-white accessories and her show number fixed around her neck on a piece of elastic. I didn't have Debbie today to show me what to do. However, after my debut at Brighton the previous August, I felt confident I had got it right.

Once the judging commenced, all the exhibitors had to leave their cats in their pens. I went across to the far side of the hall to help serve on the stall. The other exhibitors now had time to kill until the results of the judging were announced around lunchtime.

We were kept busy, selling mainly cat toys and treats. One lady browsing on our stall was looking bedraggled from the rain, her hair hanging in limp strands. Roger couldn't resist pulling her leg by offering her a cat comb to tidy her hair. Unfortunately, the lady seemed to lack a sense of humour because she was not amused by Roger's joke. She just glared at him and walked off in a huff without buying anything.

I was thrilled when Tia came first in her open class. However, the judge's decision to withhold the challenge certificate was a disappointment. Obviously, the judge didn't consider her worthy enough to award it. She did well in her side classes, making me very proud. I displayed her rosettes on the front of her pen, just as I had done at Brighton.

The general public was allowed into the hall during the afternoon, and our stall did a steady trade. However, the numerous cumbersome bags of cat litter we had brought to the show didn't sell, so we had to heave them back into the van at the end of the afternoon.

It was early evening when we drove back to the shop in the relentless rain. Linda had closed the shop and gone home. We unloaded Roger's van and replaced the unsold stock on the shelves.

Before leaving, I checked the shop's takings, which Linda had left on my desk. To my dismay, they were shockingly low, less than half of what we usually make on a Saturday. I was puzzled by this sudden, unexpected drop. Even the money we made at the cat show couldn't fully compensate for the loss at the shop. What had gone wrong? I was determined to find out from Linda on Monday morning what had caused this devastating loss.

On Sunday afternoon, Joan called me, sounding excited. She was bursting with joy as she shared the news that Stella was pregnant.

"Her artificial insemination program was successful – she is over the moon! Thank goodness it worked on the first attempt since it cost an awful lot of money."

I was genuinely happy for Stella and Mick; I couldn't be more thrilled.

Monday morning, I asked Linda to explain what had gone wrong on Saturday.

She sighed. "As you know, it rained hard all day, putting the customers off from coming out to the shops. I've never known it so quiet on a Saturday," she declared. The bad weather had significantly impacted my business; I could hardly believe how much it had adversely affected the takings.

April arrived, and the weather began to improve. However, unlike the weather, the takings didn't significantly improve. Overall, they remained low, which made for a worrying situation.

The 15th of April marked the sad passing of Tommy Cooper. It happened to be the only time I watched the Sunday evening show on the television, 'Live at Her Majesty's Theatre', and saw him collapse on stage during his act and die of a heart attack. He was one of Dad's favourite comedians, along with Eric Morecambe.

I arrived at the shop one morning to find a horrendous, gory sight confronting me. During the night, the gerbils, housed in a large cage on a shelf in the shop, had been fighting. Blood was splattered around the cage. They usually got along well together, but something must have sparked a ferocious fight, leaving dead or half-dead gerbils lying in pools of blood.

Linda walked in, and I quickly dispatched her to fetch the butcher from further along the parade. He was adept at painlessly killing sick birds by breaking their necks with a flick of his fingers. He didn't mind performing this service for us, doing it in the blink of an eye.

Now, I needed his expertise to dispense with the half-dead gerbils who were beyond help. The few remaining healthy gerbils were quickly transferred to another cage.

I was surprised by Linda's calmness at the distressing sight. "I have known them to do this occasionally," she admitted. "I don't know what sets them off, but they will fight to the death." She carried the blood-splattered cage out to the storeroom to clean it. Then she made us a much-needed recuperative coffee before we opened the shop.

Easter weekend arrived, and I was relieved to shut the shop for a couple of days. Linda would be coming in to feed the birds and animals while I took a welcome break.

I was still seeing Doug now and then when we would usually meet for a drink at a pub. He was keen for us to get away for a couple of days, so he offered to tow my caravan to the coast on Easter Day.

Saturday evening, we loaded the caravan with food and bedding, ready for our trip the next day. Byron was excited at the prospect of a short holiday by the sea.

I cooked a chicken to take with us, but while making sandwiches for the journey, Doug confessed that he didn't eat bread, leaving me at a loss to know what to pack for him.

Our destination was Durdle Door in Dorset, which held fond memories from a previous trip with Joan and Cyril.

The campsite, perched on the cliffs, offered stunning views of the iconic Durdle Door stone arch. The sight of the arch, gracefully stepping into the waves, was awe-inspiring.

Doug borrowed an Austin Maxi from his garage. It had a tow bar and was powerful enough to tow the caravan. I arranged for my brother to feed the cats while we were away.

We set off Sunday morning, and all went well for the first hour. Then, the car started to play up. It wasn't running correctly, and Doug didn't seem to know what was wrong.

We pulled into a lay-by for lunch and allowed the engine to cool down. Then we set off again with Doug gingerly coaxing the engine through the gears. It wasn't a happy engine, but we eventually arrived at the campsite on the clifftop and parked the caravan in a good position.

Doug discovered the battery wasn't holding a charge. This meant we must leave the campsite early the next day to allow plenty of time to reach home before nightfall when the headlights would be needed. All in all, it was a pretty useless car he had borrowed.

But now that we had arrived at Durdle Door, we made the most of our time there. We walked down the steep path to the beach and played football with Byron.

The chicken made an easy, tasty meal that evening while we gazed out the caravan window at the magnificent sea views. Doug remembered to bring a bottle of whisky, his favourite tipple.

Since we couldn't drive the car because we would need to use the headlights, we opted for a game of cards before turning in for the night. Byron slept at the far end in a bunk bed, curtained off, while we made up a bed by converting the seating area in the lounge.

The next morning, after a fry-up for breakfast, we went for a stroll along the clifftop towards Lulworth Cove. We needed to return to the caravan for lunch and then get it ready and hitched up for the long drive home so that we would arrive before sundown.

As we drove back, Doug had to maintain a leisurely pace to prevent the car from acting up. We made a brief stop to rest the engine before the final stretch. We made it home just as the daylight was fading. I felt relieved that the car had successfully managed the journey despite the ominous noises coming from the engine.

Spending a longer time with Doug made me realise I was becoming a little bored with his company. The car fiasco hadn't helped, and I could tell that Byron wasn't particularly impressed with him either.

As I said goodbye, I thanked Doug for taking us to the coast but decided I wouldn't be going on any more dates with him.

I returned to work the following day feeling refreshed after the brief Easter break. Lunchtime arrived, and Linda walked along the parade to the Italian cafe for our bacon sandwiches.

While she was gone, a man with a mischievous glint in his eye came into the shop carrying an umbrella. He laid it on the counter and then made an odd request. "Do you stock tortie trolleys?"

I was puzzled; I had no idea what he was asking for. "What on earth is a tortie trolley?" I demanded.

The man smiled, looking surprised. "You've not heard of a tortie trolley? They're for tortoises – they get tortoises to their destination quicker. They were widely used during World War Two in the African desert for undercover missions."

"Tortoises on trolleys?" I scoffed in disbelief; the sheer absurdity of the man's claim made me want to burst into laughter. "You're pulling my leg!" I said, unable to contain my amusement.

The man's smile widened, and he seemed to enjoy my reaction. "They were used for carrying messages in the desert," he asserted earnestly.

105

Just then, Linda returned with our sandwiches. I asked her if she had ever heard of tortie trolleys. Like me, she was totally mystified. "I've never heard of them," she declared with a puzzled frown. "Whatever they are, we definitely don't stock them - and never have!"

The man laughed and held up his hands. "OK, I'll come clean. This is just a wind-up for the local radio station."

"I don't believe you," I said. "Prove it."

The man partially opened his brolly and pulled out a microphone. "You have been live on local radio. Say hello to our listeners."

Both Linda and I were gobsmacked. At the time, I didn't find his prank particularly amusing. "You've got a right cheek, coming in here and trying to make fools of us with your ridiculous story," I told him.

The man mumbled an apology, grabbed his brolly, and beat a hasty exit. However, after he had gone, we both burst into laughter. With hindsight, I could see the funny side of his odd request, and Linda found the incident hilarious.

Later that week, I arrived at the shop one morning before Linda. I was shocked to discover the cockatiels had escaped during the night. They had been flying around the shop, knocking things off the shelves and creating utter chaos, leaving a trail of destruction in their wake. The floor was covered in a mess with broken bottles scattered around and demolished stock. I noticed the queue of people at the bus stop outside, peering through the windows. They had been entertained by the cockatiels' antics.

I felt uncomfortable under the amused gaze of the onlookers as I grabbed a fishing net and began the frantic task of recapturing the cockatiels. Linda eventually arrived full of apologies for her lateness, claiming her motorbike had broken down. We eventually managed to corral the elusive birds back into their cage after a tense and chaotic struggle, relieved to finally get the situation under control.

The shop looked as if a mini tornado had swept through. It took us quite a while to restore order, tidy up, and dispose of the broken items.

Now that May had arrived, Tia, in her second season, began her loud calls for a mate. The time had come to find a suitable stud cat for her. I decided to search for a seal point boy, hoping she would have seal point kittens in her litter.

I found a seal point stud advertised in the Cats magazine I now subscribed to, as it gave the full judges' reports from the shows. However, he was located quite a distance away on Canvey Island. Nevertheless, I rang the lady, and arranged to take Tia there at the weekend.

Upon arriving at the lady's house, I was concerned to discover that she also bred Dobermanns in addition to Colourpoint Persians. The cattery was adjacent to the kennels, and the cacophony of barking dogs immediately put a halt to Tia's urges to be mated. She was understandably frightened, and the unfamiliar place with its noisy, large dogs overwhelmed her.

The lady insisted Tia would be fine after adjusting to her new surroundings. She put Tia in a pen, and I made a fuss of her, hoping she would settle down.

I hated leaving her there, but the lady assured me Tia would soon calm down and be ready to mate.

Over the next few days, I rang the lady daily to check up on Tia, but the news wasn't good. She remained unsettled, eating nothing, and had gone off her call. I decided to collect her and give up trying to have her mated on this call. I just wanted her home again, where she would be happy, safely away from the noisy dogs.

When I collected Tia, the lady informed me that maiden queens kept as pets in the house were always tricky to get mated. However, I was sure the noisy dogs were to blame, scaring Tia and causing her to stop calling.

With the arrival of the warmer weather, Pedro enjoyed sitting in his cage outside on the bench next to the shop door, basking in the attention he received from passers-by. He had become quite a well-known celebrity among the local population. His rascally chatter and noises never failed to bring a smile to people's faces and sometimes led to amusing misunderstandings.

He often teased the girls passing by, giving them a piercing wolf whistle. The girls, unsuspecting of Pedro's mischief, would turn and wave to the builders working up on the scaffolding of the building opposite, completely unaware that it was Pedro, not the builders, who was the source of the whistling.

With summer around the corner and people considering economical holidays, I decided the time was right to sell the caravan. It seemed such a waste, sitting unused on my drive when a family could be making good use of it.

I had made all new curtains and covers for it. When I first inherited the caravan from Joan and Cyril, my brother had replaced the damaged, leaking roof, so it now looked in good condition. I couldn't help feeling a little sorry to see the caravan go, as it held many precious memories of happy holidays when Joan and Cyril owned it.

I advertised the caravan in the local newspaper and soon had some interest. A man called one Sunday to look it over and pronounced that the caravan would suit him and his family just fine, so he bought it without further ado. I felt sad to see it towed away, but I knew I had made the right decision.

On a busy Saturday, a man came into the shop accompanied by a handsome golden retriever. He asked for a thermometer so that he could take his dog's temperature. I wasn't sure whether we had any in stock, so I called out, asking Linda, who was around the corner by the fish tanks, trying to net some goldfish for another customer.

"Oh, yes, I'm sure we have," she called back. "I'll bring you one in just a minute." Linda eventually emerged from the passageway around the corner, gaily waving a fish tank thermometer measuring six inches long by an inch wide. The man's mouth dropped open in disbelief, and a look of horror spread across his face, which I found highly amusing.

"Er, Linda, this gentleman wants a thermometer for his dog," I explained, trying to suppress a giggle.

She burst out laughing. "This one would make your poor dog's eyes water," she remarked cheekily. The man soon recovered from his initial shock and chuckled at Linda's mistake, his sense of humour restored.

Unfortunately, that was the only type of thermometer we currently stocked. I assured the man I would order some dog thermometers and have them in stock by the following week.

On the 28th of May, the newscaster delivered a piece of news that saddened us all. The second of Dad's favourite comedians, Eric Morecambe, had passed away suddenly from a heart attack, his third in sixteen years. After the success of his and Ernie Wise's Christmas shows, he would be greatly missed by the whole nation.

The hot weather was causing problems at the shop. I was serving a lady customer, weighing out loose dog biscuits from the large bin that stood against the wall beside the counter, when, to my horror, I noticed insects crawling around amongst the biscuits. I yelled for Linda and pointed into the bin.

"Oh, we get them in the dog biscuits at this time of year," she whispered so the customer wouldn't hear. "They're weevils. Don't worry, I'll pick them out."

I shuddered at Linda's words and then finished serving the customer, ensuring no weevils were in the bag of biscuits I handed her.

Linda carefully removed all the weevils from the dog biscuits, being discreet if customers were in the shop. Then, she started inspecting the jars of various birdseeds lined up on the shelf above the bins.

"What are you doing, Linda?" I asked suspiciously, peering over her shoulder.

"The warm weather can also cause maggots to appear in the birdseed," she said as she removed the lid from a jar and shook the contents, looking for movement. "Yes, just as I suspected. There they are, wriggling around." She sounded unconcerned.

"Ugh! How revolting!" I exclaimed. "Please take the jars into the backyard and dispose of the seed."

My pet shop was turning into a house of horrors, with cockroaches and an enormous spider lurking in the storeroom, weevils and maggots in the dog biscuits and birdseed. The gerbils massacring each other in the dead of night, not to mention Pete, the ghost, who inexplicably moved things around. Linda had recently lost her hairbrush only to discover it hidden amongst the bags of meat in the freezer. She was certain that Pete, the ghost, was responsible.

However, the shop had even more worrying surprises for me as I was closing up one evening after Linda had left. Just as I was about to head home, a large hamster caught my eye, scurrying across the floor from the bins and disappearing behind the chest freezer. I leaned over the freezer and peered behind it. I could see a hole in the skirting board, evidently the hamster's escape route.

I checked the hamster cages on the shelf in the shop and could find no missing hamsters or an open door where one might have escaped. Puzzled, I decided to get Linda to recheck the hamsters in the morning in case I had miscounted them.

When I told Linda about the hamster the next morning, she made a shocking revelation. "What you saw was a wild hamster," she asserted. "They are happily living and breeding behind the skirting boards."

"What!" I gasped, horrified by Linda's words. "Can't we capture them? They must be pet hamsters that have escaped."

Linda laughed. "Well, they might have been pets once, but they're certainly not pets anymore. They have grown big and strong and would probably bite your finger off if you were able to handle one. They have got the ideal habitat here. At night, they come out and help themselves to the loose hamster food in the bin. They fill their cheek pouches, then return to their nests behind the skirting boards."

"We can't allow them to run rampant, breeding unchecked. It'll be a hamster invasion, almost as bad as a rat infestation!" I was deeply concerned by this situation, which I could foresee escalating into a serious problem. I insisted we must try to capture them.

I carefully lowered a couple of humane traps into position behind the freezer, near the hole, hoping a hamster would be tempted to enter the trap for the food and find itself caught as the door snapped shut behind it. I kept an empty cage handy nearby, ready to house any captured hamsters.

However, my attempts were met with no success. When I checked the traps each morning, they were disappointingly empty, as if the hamsters were mocking my efforts.

One Saturday afternoon, when Byron was busy cleaning out the animal cages in the shop, I spotted a bold hamster darting behind the counter, heading for the rear of the freezer. Determined to catch it, I grabbed a fishing net and leaned over the freezer, but the hole was just out of reach. I yelled for Byron to come and help, knowing his smaller size would give him an advantage.

Then Linda joined us. Seeing Byron struggling to reach the hole with the net, she quickly grabbed one of his legs, so I grabbed the other one. Byron let out a surprised yell as he found himself suspended upside down behind the freezer. But at least now, he could reach the hole. Suddenly, a fat hamster dashed out of the hole, and Byron managed to scoop it up in the net.

We hauled him out, and Linda took charge of the net. Realising it was caught, the frantic hamster attempted to gnaw its way out. Meanwhile, I quickly grabbed the empty cage.

As Linda carefully transferred the ferocious hamster to the cage, a lady entered the shop. She was curious to know what we were doing. I reluctantly explained that we were catching hamsters that were living wild in the shop.

A look of horror crossed the lady's face, and she let out a piercing scream. In one swift movement, she leapt onto the chair beside the counter with an agility that surprised me, her eyes warily scanning the floor. I tried to calm her down, assuring her that the hamsters were harmless.

Meanwhile, the captured hamster was venting its fury on the cage's metal bars, blatantly proving me to be lying. It had all four feet braced against the bars, gnashing at them with such ferocity that I feared the cage wouldn't withstand the onslaught.

From her vantage point on the chair, the nervous lady witnessed the hamster going berserk. With a startled shriek, she leapt down and made a dash for the door.

Linda quickly removed the cage to the back room before any more customers saw the savage hamster.

"Do you think that hamster will ever tame down?" I asked Linda when she returned to the shop.

"I very much doubt it," she surmised. "We couldn't sell it, even if it did calm down, because we don't know how old it is."

I nodded. "Yes, that one is a fully-grown adult. Customers expect to buy baby hamsters, not huge muscle-bound ones. I just hope the bars of that cage can hold out against the onslaught from that one."

Linda chuckled. "Their free lifestyle behind the skirting boards certainly seems to suit them so much better than spending their life cooped up in a cage."

I sighed. "All we can do is keep these hamsters caged in the back room as we capture them since they're unsaleable."

"Well, if any are pregnant, then at least we'll have some baby hamsters to sell," Linda pointed out, trying to cheer me up by adding a little hope to the situation.

"I doubt that terrified lady who has just run out of the shop will ever return, so that's one customer we've lost," I said ruefully.

The following week, the owner of the haberdashery shop next door came in looking vexed.

"I have just discovered some hamsters running around in my shop," he declared. "They have obviously come through from your pet shop. I can't have hamsters chewing at my merchandise. I need some traps to catch them."

I apologised and handed him some of the humane traps. I tried to reassure him that the traps would soon catch any hamsters loose in his shop. However, I secretly harboured doubts since our traps hadn't succeeded so far.

Chapter Six

Daffy Duck

Linda arrived one morning with some worrying news. "There's a new pet shop just opened in the High Street," she announced, sounding concerned.

This news struck me like a bolt of lightning. Alarm bells began ringing in my ears, amplifying the sense of urgency. "But that means they'll be in direct competition with my shop!" I exclaimed in dismay, my heart sinking at the thought of the difficult situation this would inevitably create.

"They have three other branches in nearby towns, so they are well-established," Linda informed me. This was the last thing I needed to hear after the takings had been dropping since March.

"How about I send my younger brother, Jason, to this new shop to case the joint? I'll get him to make a note of a few prices so we can compare them to ours," Linda suggested.

"That's a good idea. Knowing what sort of competition we're up against will be helpful."

The next day, Jason called in on his way home from school. He told us he had just been into the new pet shop and had jotted down some prices. He handed me a scrap of paper with a list of items scrawled on it.

"I hope you were discreet and didn't arouse any suspicions," I told him.

He looked a little uncomfortable. "Er, well, the man serving in the shop did ask what I was doing, so I pretended I wanted to buy a dog collar, and then I made the excuse that I didn't know the right size."

The following morning, a man entered the shop and introduced himself as the manager of the new pet shop in the High Street.

"I'd appreciate it if you didn't send your assistant's brother to my shop to spy on what we are stocking," he said curtly.

"What!" I gasped, feigning shocked surprise. He had caught me off guard, but I quickly decided the best form of defence was attack. "I would never dream of asking anyone to do that," I retorted, glaring at him. "It's of no interest to me what you stock."

"Well, I don't want to see him in my shop again!" the man declared and then stomped out.

Linda came into the shop from the back room. She had heard the man's cross voice, so I told her about my unpleasant visitor. She looked surprised. "I wonder how he knew Jason was my brother."

"You'd better warn him that he's barred from that shop. Now that I come to think about it, that man looked familiar. I'm sure I saw him staring in our window last week on a couple of occasions. I bet he was checking up on his competition. What a hypocrite!"

Once I'd had a chance to study the figures Jason had jotted down, I was shocked to discover that most items were being sold at cost price, obviously with the intention of putting me out of business.

When I showed the figures to Linda, she agreed. "He can afford to do that because he's got the other branches to keep him going."

The realisation that a shopkeeper was willing to act so ruthlessly to close down a competitor's business was a shock. I felt as if I had been stabbed in the back, a betrayal I had naively never anticipated in the business world. With the shop struggling to make a reasonable turnover, I had to give up having Wundapets deliver my orders. Instead, by going to the warehouse and buying directly with cash and carry, I could get goods that little bit cheaper. I also had a card that gave me access to another, even larger warehouse at Greenwich, which sold a wider range of goods.

In addition to the pet food and accessories on offer, I couldn't resist some of the treats in the grocery section. I returned to the shop with a large box of KitKats for Linda and me to enjoy with our coffee. Storing them in the freezer kept them cool during the warm weather.

Linda told me about another tempting treat at the baker's shop, conveniently located across the road. Just before closing time, they offered their remaining delectable cream cakes at a fraction of the price. She found this treat hard to resist and often returned with a bagful of these sweet delights, some to take home for her family.

Among the shop's diverse hamster collection, including Russian, golden and ruby-eyed cinnamon, I was particularly drawn to the silky and long-coated varieties. The idea of cross-breeding them to create a unique, silky, long-coated hamster was intriguing.

With the space in the back room already taken up with breeding Dutch and Newfoundland Dwarf rabbits, smooth-coated and Abyssinian guinea pigs, hamsters and gerbils, I took a couple of suitable hamsters home with me, keeping them in separate cages in Byron's bedroom, away from the cats, until the time was right to mate them.

Byron enjoyed having them to play with in the meantime. However, he had to be careful if they were running around in his bedroom, to make sure his bedroom door was closed so that Jojo couldn't get near them because, with his feral roots, he would only view them as a tasty meal.

Nature took its course, and a litter of hamsters eventually arrived. Among them were the much-desired silky, long-coated baby hamsters. They proved to be very popular with my customers.

Summer was getting into full swing, and work at the shop was mounting up. I had taken in a litter of lively black mongrel puppies to find them loving homes. The extra work involved in caring for them and keeping their pen clean was a labour of love.

Daffy Duck arrived to be boarded for two weeks. I was honouring Anne's arrangement to board her while her owners took a holiday. Anne had sold a whole batch of ducklings and goslings to local residents on this understanding.

Linda was accustomed to having Daffy come in for boarding. "She's very partial to lettuce," Linda informed me, "so I'll pop along the parade to the greengrocer and get her a fresh lettuce each morning as a daily treat."

Daffy became well-known amongst my regular customers as she happily waddled around the shop, quacking loudly. The only problem was the mess she squirted onto the floor. Linda or I would quickly clean it up before it got trodden in. However, sometimes, if we were busy, it didn't get cleaned up soon enough, and we'd discover a footprint or a skid mark!

We kept a galvanised bath in the back room filled with water so she could enjoy a limited swim. She had a nest in a cage on the floor beneath a shelf where she laid an egg most days. I looked forward to the novelty of a delicious fresh duck egg for tea.

At home, I was still looking for a suitable stud cat for Tia. She would soon be calling again, and I needed to find her a stud cat, preferably local. I placed an advert in the paper, which produced a promising reply.

A lady from West Dartford rang me and introduced herself as Mrs Burnell. She offered her stud cat's services, stipulating that it was only because Tia was a maiden. The lady didn't normally allow her cat to be used at public stud.

She described him, and he sounded perfect. The only slight downside was his colour. He was a blue tabby-point, so there would be no seal point kittens, and with no visible tabby-points on Tia's side of the pedigree, there would probably be no tabby-point kittens either.

I arranged to take Tia to Mrs Burnell's house once she was calling again. I took the precaution of checking that there were no dogs on the premises to put Tia off. Mrs Burnell assured me she only had a few cats in a small breeding cattery, which sounded ideal.

The day arrived when I took Tia to West Dartford to be mated. I finally got to meet the elderly Mrs Burnell. Her years of experience and expertise in cat breeding were immediately evident as she made a fuss of Tia and introduced me to her stud cat. I was very impressed by the large, handsome boy with a good type and friendly disposition.

"He's a gentle giant," she assured me. "He's accustomed to being patient with maiden queens who are often more difficult to get mated."

I settled Tia in an adjoining run so the two cats could get acquainted through the netting that separated them. This was a crucial step in the mating process, allowing the cats to become familiar with each other's scent and presence before the actual mating.

"When I think they are ready, I'll try putting them in the one run, and of course, I'll be supervising their mating," Mrs Burnell explained.

I was happy to entrust Tia to her for the next few days, knowing Tia would be in capable hands. Mrs Burnell's experience reassured me that Tia would be well cared for.

After several days, I received a phone call from Mrs Burnell to tell me she wasn't having any luck getting Tia mated. She suggested keeping Tia there for a few weeks until her next call, if necessary, so she would be entirely at ease by then. As much as I was missing Tia, I realised it was the only solution to get her mated, so I reluctantly agreed.

One Saturday evening, I had an unexpected visit from Mrs Bullinaire and her son, Colin. They were our ex-neighbours from the Crescent whom our family had known for years and remained friends with after they moved away. Two years ago, I visited my long-time friend, Katy, Colin's older sister, while staying in Norfolk with Joan and Cyril.

Pedro was home for the weekend, sitting on his perch in his cage. Mrs Bullinaire and Colin were fascinated by him as he rattled off some of the phrases in his repertoire. Mrs Bullinaire was well-known for her ability to produce piercing whistles. She started whistling to Pedro, who was quick to mimic whatever whistles she made. Mrs Bullinaire found this hilarious. Her laughter set Pedro off with his belly laugh. He rocked to and fro on his perch while Mrs Bullinaire laughed so much she toppled off the sofa.

Colin, Byron, and I watched in amusement the comical scene confronting us: Mrs Bullinaire sprawled on the floor, laughing helplessly, and Pedro, rocking on his perch, joining in with his belly laugh.

"Oh, he's priceless!" Mrs Bullinaire gasped, picking herself up off the floor. "I'd love to have a pet like him, but I wouldn't get any work done because I'd be too busy talking and whistling to him all day long."

After several weeks of trying to get Tia mated, Mrs Burnell admitted defeat and arranged for me to collect Tia. I was disappointed but pleased to have her back home again.

"I've tried really hard with her," Mrs Burnell declared as she helped to secure Tia in her basket. "Unfortunately, she has remained homesick and missing you. Some queens never get mated because they are so spoilt at home."

I had to admit that I did spoil her. "Perhaps I shall have to give up and just let her be a pampered pet."

"Well, there is one way that is fairly foolproof," Mrs Burnell told me. "Just get your own stud cat for Tia."

"But a stud cat needs at least three queens to keep him happy," I pointed out. "Also, he must have his own quarters once he becomes adult and starts spraying."

"I was in a similar dilemma to you with my first queen – that was when I decided to get my own stud, and it has worked out very well."

Mrs Burnell confessed that she would love to take her boy to cat shows and try to get him made up to a champion. "I think he's good enough to win his class and get a challenge certificate," she said. "Unfortunately, I have no transport to get to the shows."

"I can always give you a lift if I'm going to a show," I offered.

Mrs Burnell beamed with delight. "I might take you up on your kind offer."

I arrived home with my head in a whirl. Should I take Mrs Burnell's advice and acquire my own stud cat? I hadn't even considered this an option until now. I needed to work out whether it could be a practical solution. If I bought a kitten, it would be another year before he matured into a stud cat. I had read that a stud cat's first experience ought to be with an experienced queen. Likewise, a maiden queen's first mating should be with an experienced stud. What I was considering was the exact opposite. Still, Mrs Burnell's advice had sounded encouraging, giving me food for thought.

During a brief coffee break in the pet shop, I discussed the falling turnover with Linda.

"I need to come up with a way of boosting the sales. Do you have any ideas, Linda?"

"What about your plan to diversify into tropical fish? You wanted to convert part of the storeroom to accommodate them."

I sighed. "Unfortunately, there just isn't sufficient money available to do the work. I'm already struggling to pay the rent on the shop, and I've cut back on lines that aren't selling well. The main problem is that new pet shop on the High Street taking my business. I can't afford to compete with them by slashing my prices to cost price or below."

Linda nodded. "They're lucky that they can rely on their other branches to keep this branch viable."

"I'll display a notice offering free local delivery. It could be helpful, especially on the bulky items we sell, like the bags of peat, compost and cat litter. Hopefully, this service will appeal to our customers. I'm also considering staying open on Wednesday afternoons. I believe this could potentially create a little more business, as most of the other shops in this parade and on the High Street close for a half-day on Wednesdays. Do you think it could be a constructive move for us?"

"I suppose it could generate a little more income," Linda said, trying to be supportive.

"While I don't really want to give up my time off on a Wednesday, I'm willing to make sacrifices to improve the takings. Desperate times call for desperate measures! Starting this week, I'll stay open all day on Wednesdays and see if it helps to boost the figures."

Over the next few weeks, I kept the shop open on Wednesday afternoons after Linda had gone home. However, I soon discovered that the shop remained depressingly empty of customers. The few who did come in to stock up with food for their pets no longer needed to come in towards the end of the week, so the overall weekly takings weren't increasing.

I had hoped these extended opening times would be a solution, but I was wrong. My experiment was an unmitigated failure, leaving me feeling frustrated and depressed, taking a toll on my morale and enthusiasm for the business.

I received an unexpected visit from my Auntie Con and Uncle Alf. They had just returned from a once-in-a-lifetime holiday in South Africa, visiting their youngest son, Desmond, who worked in a high-powered job at one of the principal diamond mines.

Con was Mum's youngest sister and my favourite aunt. They lived on the coast near Blackpool but had come to stay with Mum and Dad for a few days. We spent an enjoyable evening hearing all about their experiences and safaris, illustrated with numerous photos.

I managed to steer the conversation away from my troubles at the pet shop, knowing my Uncle Alf was a born worrier who suffered from ulcers. I didn't want to give him any additional cause to worry.

Despite the depressingly low turnover at the pet shop, there were the occasional brighter moments when a customer's desire for a custom-made large aquarium led to a sudden boost in the takings. With the help of a trusted contact, I could fulfil this request, providing the customer with a high-quality tank. I found this very rewarding, especially when the customer requested all the accessories and an assortment of fish to complement the aquarium.

This was the added benefit of selling livestock, as each sale could snowball if the customer also needed a cage, food and accessories. At least I did have this advantage over the pet shop on the High Street, which didn't accommodate livestock.

Thanks to Pedro's captivating antics, we occasionally received requests for a parrot, usually a blue-fronted Amazon like Pedro, or a handsome cockatoo or a magnificent macaw. These birds were not only very expensive but also quite rare, making them a luxury item.

Linda informed me that Anne had usually kept one or two for sale in the shop, whereas I could only afford to sell them to order.

One evening, Shelley rang to invite me to a brass party she was holding. Similar to a Tupperware party, this gathering was a pleasing departure from the usual, showcasing brass ornaments and utensils as the main attraction. It made a welcome break from the daily worries at the pet shop.

The small lounge was crowded with women, mostly Shelley's work colleagues. Her mum, Gwen, and her aunt were also there.

Roger arrived home halfway through the evening, feeling hungry. He wanted to make a sandwich, but the only loaf of bread was in the freezer. Undeterred, Roger set up his Workmate bench in the middle of the kitchen, clamped the loaf, and produced a large saw from his toolbox. He proceeded to saw through the frozen loaf, much to the amusement of Shelley's surprised guests, who found his unorthodox method of slicing bread quite entertaining.

Shelley had coffee or tea with assorted cakes laid out for her guests. A lot of light-hearted chattering ensued while we sorted through the brass knick-knacks.

I found it hard to resist the allure of the brass ornaments, so I came home with a jug and a large, embossed plate.

Always looking for cost-saving measures in the shop, I came up with the idea of supplying the fish tanks with oxygenating pond weed from my garden pond. The pond, choked with weed, now became an added source of income, albeit only making a small contribution.

Linda was tasked with cleaning the weed in the sink and then bunching it, secured with a lead tie, to keep it upright on the floor of the fish tanks. The weed sold well, as I could afford to keep the price low. However, it made little impact on our overall takings.

On July 19th, an unusual magnitude 5.4 earthquake, with its epicentre on the Welsh Llynn Peninsular, sent shock waves throughout the UK.

I received my own set of shock waves when I discovered the shop hadn't made sufficient profit to meet the quarterly rent that was now due. I was also in arrears on the bank loan, receiving demanding letters from the bank manager that gave me sleepless nights.

I rang the freeholder of the shop and explained my predicament, hoping to be given some leeway, but I was met with disappointment. Apparently, he wasn't willing to cooperate.

This was the final straw. I had to face up to the fact that the shop was no longer a viable commercial enterprise. The competitive pet shop in the High Street had succeeded in ruining my already struggling business. I reluctantly concluded that I had no option but to put the shop on the market.

When I broke the bad news to Linda, she was saddened by my decision, which wasn't entirely unexpected. She had witnessed the decline in our customer numbers, even on busy Saturdays when a queue had once stretched from the counter at the back of the shop to the front door. Long queues were now a thing of the past. The emotional toll of this decline was heavy on both of us, as we had tried hard to make the shop work. The realisation that our efforts were not enough was painful.

"What will you do once the shop is sold?" Linda asked as I checked the till at the end of another quiet day.

"I did warn Byron that if the shop didn't work out, we would have no choice but to sell up and move to Norfolk. Our bungalow will need to be sold to repay the outstanding rent and the bank loan because the sale of the shop won't cover all the debts."

The thought of leaving my comfortable bungalow, which held so many memories, was depressing.

"At least properties in Norfolk are a lot cheaper than in Kent, so I should still be able to afford a decent place once I've repaid all the debts this shop has incurred. I'm hoping for a fresh start in a new location."

"But what will you do for work in Norfolk?" Linda asked, sounding concerned.

I shrugged. "I haven't thought that far ahead. I would love to breed Colourpoint Persians, but I'm not sure how feasible that would be. I only have Tia at the moment, and so far, I haven't managed to get her mated."

The following day, I contacted an agency that dealt with commercial properties. I arranged for them to come and take down all the particulars and measurements, ready for marketing the pet shop. I deliberately avoided using the Gibraltar agency, knowing the sexual harassment I would undoubtedly receive from randy John.

Byron and I were invited to Sunday lunch with my parents, so I took this opportunity to tell them of my plans.

They had been aware for some time now that I was struggling to make ends meet at the shop. Therefore, my decision to sell came as no surprise to them. I suspected they were a little relieved, as they had shown some reservations when I initially told them of my intention to buy the shop.

I had already explained the situation to Byron. He was far from happy at the prospect of uprooting from the area he had grown up in, leaving his secondary school and all his friends. He was clearly troubled by the thought of such a significant change in his life.

I fully empathised with him, understanding that thirteen is a challenging age for a teenager, let alone starting afresh in a new location and attending a new secondary school where he would know no one. It pained me to see him in this situation. Still, I felt I had no choice because I had to sell my lovely little bungalow to become solvent again.

We enjoyed a delicious Sunday roast, which we ate in the lounge. The dining table had been moved there to make room for Dad's bed in the dining room, as nowadays he has difficulty climbing the stairs.

Afterwards, we relaxed over a cup of tea, and I discussed our plans for the big move to Norfolk once the shop was sold.

Then, Dad dropped a bombshell out of the blue. "If you and Byron are moving to Norfolk, then so am I!" he announced emphatically.

Mum looked at him in surprise. She obviously hadn't been consulted about this unexpected turn of events. Yet, to my utter amazement, Mum just smiled and agreed with Dad's sudden proposal.

They had lived in the Crescent for over thirty-five years. This move to Norfolk would be an even bigger upheaval for them in their retirement years than for me and Byron. Nevertheless, I was overjoyed that they were resolute in their decision to accompany us.

"We don't need this three-bedroom house; now it's just the two of us living here," Dad reasoned. "If we pool our resources, we can search for a property with a granny annexe large enough to accommodate your mum and me."

"Or we could look for a pair of bungalows, maybe semi-detached, to buy – one for each of us," Mum suggested as she warmed to the idea of living in Norfolk. She was born and bred in Suffolk, so it would be like returning to her roots. She still had several relatives and friends living in Suffolk and Norfolk.

Byron brightened up a little at the prospect of his grandparents accompanying us on the big move. Their excitement and optimism about this new adventure gave my spirits an unexpected boost, which I found reassuring.

"I wonder what Roger will make of his entire family upping sticks and moving to Norfolk," I mused with a smile.

"Perhaps he and Shelley will consider a similar move; after all, they don't really have any ties in Dartford, apart from Shelley's family," Mum said. Roger had always been the apple of her eye, so I knew she would be delighted if he moved to Norfolk, too.

Being self-employed as a carpenter and window fitter, it wouldn't be too difficult for Roger to set up his business in a new area. However, Shelley was definitely a townie – she loved shopping. One day away from shops would give her withdrawal symptoms, so she could be a fly in the ointment if Roger did decide to swap town living for a rural lifestyle in Norfolk.

My parents were keen to put their house on the market as soon as possible. I realised that selling the shop, my bungalow, and my parents' house and finding suitable properties for us in Norfolk could take a considerable time.

I wasn't ready to put my bungalow on the market. First, I needed to redecorate and repair the wallpaper where Pedro had torn strips off the wall. I could only do this during the evenings or on Sundays, so I knew it would take a while before the bungalow was ready for an agent to take photos and arrange viewings.

The following week, I had a surprise at the shop when a couple brought in a young pedigree Pekinese named Benji. They wanted me to find him a new home because they felt they couldn't care for him properly when they were both at work all day.

It was clearly a difficult decision for the couple, and I couldn't help but sympathise. They explained that they both had demanding jobs that kept them out of the house for long hours, and they felt it was unfair on Benji to leave him alone for so long. Despite my initial reluctance, I agreed to take care of Benji and find him a good home.

Pekinese weren't a favourite breed of mine, with their bulging eyes and squashed faces, sometimes causing breathing problems. However, I found myself drawn to this little dog. Something about his timid demeanour and large, sad eyes tugged at my heartstrings.

Linda was equally smitten by him. "Isn't he cute!" she exclaimed, picking him up and cuddling him.

"Any chance that you could give him a home?" I asked hopefully, watching her fussing over him.

Linda sighed. "I wish I could, but we've already got a dog. There's no way Mum would let us have another one. How about you? You don't have a dog. I'm sure he would get along fine with your cats."

"I'm not sure, especially since I'm out all day working here." I have always preferred cats over dogs, yet I couldn't deny the unexpected appeal of owning a Pekinese.

"That's not a problem – you simply bring him to work with you. He wouldn't be in the way." Linda was succeeding in persuading me, which I found surprising.

On impulse, I said, "OK, I'll take him home and see how he gets on with the cats, but if he causes any problems, I shall have to bring him back."

I knew his coat would take quite a lot of grooming, but I was accustomed to that with Tia's coat. Pekinese have a double coat, which means they shed a lot. Regular brushing and grooming would be necessary to keep Benji's coat in good condition and prevent matting.

After work, I brought Benji home and introduced him to Jojo and Tia. They made it clear that they were the bosses in their house. Jojo growled, and Tia hissed at him, so he took refuge behind me. I had to be patient and let them get used to each other's scents and presence. They eventually came to an uneasy truce, with Benji keeping his distance from the cats.

Before going to bed, I settled Benji in his bed in the kitchen. I noticed that Benji had a rather strong doggy odour, so I planned to bath him A.S.A.P.

In the middle of the night, I suddenly awoke, unsure what had disturbed my sleep. As I opened my eyes, a pungent aroma assaulted my nose. I was horrified to find a pair of large, boggling eyes staring into my face through the darkness.

A scream escaped my lips before I had time to rationalise the situation. Then I realised it was only Benji sitting beside my bed, staring at me. Feeling lonely, he decided to come and find me. I got up and firmly put him back in his bed in the kitchen, carefully closing my bedroom door properly when I returned to bed.

The next morning, I got up and was dismayed to discover dog poo on the kitchen floor. Apparently, Benji wasn't house-trained. This was the deciding factor for me after my fright in the night. Benji would have to go. I knew I must find him a home where he would be happy and well cared for.

I took him to work and put an advert in the shop window. Being a young, pedigree Pekinese, there was plenty of interest in Benji.

After carefully vetting the various interested parties, I chose a young couple, John and Sarah, with a young daughter, Emily. Sarah stayed home all day caring for Emily, so Benji would have plenty of company. They weren't fazed when I mentioned that he wasn't yet house-trained. It was a difficult decision, but I knew it was the best for Benji when I handed him over to his new family, knowing he would be cherished.

They were over the moon with Benji and brought him back to the shop after a couple of weeks to show me how well he had adjusted to his new life. He looked like a happy, contented little dog, odour-free and clearly doted on by his new owners. Seeing him thriving in a new home, I felt relieved and reassured that I had made the right decision by not keeping Benji.

One Sunday afternoon, I stood on steps, scraping wallpaper off my bedroom wall as I prepared to redecorate the room. The phone rang – it was Dad. He wanted to see me straight away. I explained that I was busy, but he insisted it was urgent – he had to see me now.

Worried that something was wrong, I dropped everything, jumped in the car, and drove to his house. I dashed indoors and found Dad sitting at the dining table in the lounge, looking dispirited, but he brightened up as I came in.

"Whatever is the matter?" I demanded anxiously. "What do you want me for?"

Dad smiled. "Nothing's the matter. I just needed to talk to you. Your mum is out, visiting friends."

I gave a sigh of relief and sat down. "So, what's on your mind? What do you need to talk to me about?"

"Nothing in particular," Dad admitted. "I simply wanted to see you."

This was far from typical of Dad. I was touched that he wanted to see me, but I remained puzzled because he sounded desperate on the phone.

I went to the kitchen and made some tea. Then we sat and chatted for a while. I told Dad about Benji, and he agreed that I had made the right decision by re-homing him. Dad told me how much he was looking forward to living in Norfolk.

Dad had his oxygen tank beside his chair, ready in case he had one of his attacks when he couldn't catch his breath. I had witnessed one or two of these attacks, which frightened me. I hated seeing Dad struggling to breathe and gasping for air. He had been hospitalised several times when the attacks became more severe and required additional treatment.

These hospitalisations were becoming more frequent, a grim reminder that the underlying cause, his emphasaemia, was incurable.

My parents' house was now on the market. Dad told me that there had been several viewings already.

"One young couple were so keen that they offered to buy our house straight away."

"That's brilliant news, Dad," I exclaimed.

Dad shook his head. "We didn't even get as far as instructing solicitors. The agents rang to say the couple couldn't secure a mortgage. The disappointment was mutual."

"Never mind, I'm sure you'll soon find another buyer. This is a good-sized three-bedroom house in a convenient location for shops and schools," I pointed out. "Now, I must get back to my decorating; else, at this rate, I'll never get my bungalow on the market."

Jemima Goose arrived at the shop to be boarded for the next two weeks while her owners took a holiday. Like Daffy Duck, Jemima happily waddled around the shop, making a mess with her droppings. She would startle customers by honking loudly behind them. Linda made her a nest in the back room, and the galvanised bathtub, filled with water, gave her a small makeshift pond to swim in. Boarding Jemima meant I could now enjoy fresh goose eggs for tea.

Once I was satisfied that my bungalow was looking spruced and tidy, I called an estate agent to arrange for him to come and take measurements and photos in preparation for putting it on the market.

Before long, I had a viewing booked for a Sunday morning. A family arrived consisting of a young mum and dad and their seven-year-old son.

They explained that the choice of a new home hinged entirely on whether their son approved of the property because they had to make allowances for his autism. I had no idea about the complexities of autism. If their son liked the new home, that would be the deciding factor in buying the property.

The little boy's eyes lit up excitedly as I showed them around. He was already imagining himself living here and was particularly drawn to Byron's room, which would be his own room. His parents couldn't hide their smiles, a clear sign of their son's influence on their decision.

The following day, the estate agent called to say the couple and their son loved the bungalow and intended to arrange a mortgage to buy it. This was good news for me, but I still had the shop to sell, which hadn't attracted any interest.

A week later, my estate agent rang with disappointing news. The young couple, who had shown such promise, had been unable to acquire a mortgage. Despite empathising with their situation, I was back at square one, like my parents.

Chapter Seven

Hunting for a Home

Now that all three properties were on the market, I decided to spend a day in Norfolk viewing some bungalows. An agent had sent me details of properties that might suit us, so I arranged to take Mum, Dad, and Byron to see them on Sunday.

We set off early in the morning as the owners of the first bungalow were expecting us at 11 a.m. This was a modern bungalow in the village of Necton. It had an attached annexe and two acres of garden.

After a good journey with no hold-ups, we pulled up in front of the neat-looking bungalow in a street of similar bungalows. The husband and wife warmly greeted us when we knocked on the door. The wife did most of the talking as she guided us on a tour of her home.

My initial impression of the bungalow was one of blandness and lacking in character. The two double bedrooms and the lounge with an open fire were as described in the brochure, but the rooms were quite small.

The annexe, also with small rooms, including one double bedroom, seemed like a tight fit for Mum and Dad, even after downsizing. Yet, they managed to sound pleasantly surprised by what the annexe offered. I suspected they were only being polite.

The husband showed us around the two-acre garden at the rear of the bungalow. It stretched in a long, narrow strip, widening into a small field at the far end where they kept pigs and chickens. There was a well-planned vegetable plot, and the rest of the garden was laid to lawn. The husband mentioned using a ride-on mower to cut the grass, which he would be leaving.

After the tour, we were invited for coffee in the lounge. The wife, a local primary school teacher, explained that her mother had lived in the annexe before she moved to a care home.

They were planning to relocate to a nearby village but didn't give a reason for their move, and we didn't bother to ask. The wife emphasised the convenience of the village amenities, including a post office, butchers, and doctor's surgery. She pointed out that this was far more than most Norfolk villages offered.

We thanked the couple for showing us around and then drove into the nearby market town of East Dereham to get some lunch. Being a Sunday, the town was quiet. We parked outside the Otters Holt, a hotel and restaurant on Church Street. We were soon tucking into a delicious Sunday roast in the spacious restaurant.

Over our meal, we discussed the bungalow and annexe we had just viewed. Clearly, none of us were particularly taken with the property.

"The annexe was quite nice, but we would have nowhere to put our furniture," Mum said.

"You will need to dispose of most of your furniture if you are downsizing from a three-bedroom house to a one-bedroom annexe," I reminded her.

"There wasn't even room for a dining table in the lounge," Mum remarked, sounding disappointed.

I sighed. I could understand her feelings. She wasn't adjusting well to the idea of downsizing.

"No, that annexe was far too cramped for both of us," Dad declared firmly. "It might work for one person, but definitely not for two."

His concerns were valid, and I had to agree with him. "I wasn't particularly keen on the bungalow either," I admitted. Byron, who had been unusually quiet, nodded in agreement. It was clear that he was not looking forward to the move to Norfolk, and his lack of enthusiasm was noticeable.

Our next viewing in the afternoon was a pair of semi-detached bungalows in the nearby village of Lyng. At least this time, there was no granny annexe; it was a full-sized two-bedroom bungalow.

We found the bungalows in a quiet cul-de-sac. Again, they were modern, lacking the character of older properties. Elderly neighbours owned them who, coincidently, had decided to move house at the same time.

The bungalows were mirror images of each other in the layout of their rooms, both having two bedrooms. The back gardens were small, backing onto other properties, which I wasn't keen on. Mum and Dad seemed quite taken with the bungalows, but they could tell I was unimpressed.

We thanked the couples for showing us around and then started the long journey home. On the way, we discussed the pros and cons of the two semi-detached bungalows.

"I know you would prefer more garden, but you could easily create an access to our garden and make use of it as a vegetable patch if you like," Mum suggested.

"Even so, the properties are quite small, and the rear gardens are overlooked, which I really hate," I said. One thing I couldn't accept was a garden overlooked by neighbours. I valued my privacy too much.

By the time we reached home, a shared sense of disappointment in the properties had settled in. Our search for the perfect home was far from over, and the daunting prospect of finding it seemed more challenging than ever.

One quiet afternoon, Vick entered the shop, bearing news that left Linda in a state of shock. Despite the devastating nature of the news, Vick's face remained stoic, as usual, almost as if he was unable to fully process the events.

He didn't linger but went home, leaving Linda visibly distraught, needing time to process the news. She went to make some tea, her mind reeling. Clearly, she was struggling to come to terms with what she had just heard.

There were no customers, so when she returned with two mugs of tea, she confided to me what he had told her.

While driving his van, Vick didn't notice a man stepping off the pavement onto the zebra crossing in front of him. Vick had braked sharply but not in time. His van struck the man, knocking him down. By the time the man arrived at the hospital, he was pronounced dead.

Linda assured me that Vick was distraught by what had happened. There had been no way of telling by studying his face. "Vick says he'll be prosecuted and could end up going to prison over this. Fatally hitting a pedestrian on a crossing is extremely serious."

"But does Vick realise just how serious this is?" I asked. He hadn't looked upset to me despite Linda insisting he was devastated.

"This has really shaken Vick," Linda declared. "It's going to take a long time for him to come to terms with it, especially if he ends up in jail."

"I daresay the poor man's relatives are none too happy either," I remarked. Given the circumstances, I found it hard to empathise with Vick. He seemed to be not paying attention when he approached the pedestrian crossing. However, I refrained from saying so to Linda as she was obviously very worried about her boyfriend.

At home, I finally decided to follow Mrs Burnell's advice and invest in a kitten to rear as a future stud cat for Tia. I concluded that it was the only way to ever get Tia mated.

My heart was set on a seal point boy, so I eagerly scoured the adverts in my Cats magazine. I discovered one for sale, but his location was Brighton. I immediately rang the breeder and arranged to visit her on Sunday, accompanied by Byron. When I mentioned my intended trip to Mum and Dad, they were keen to come along.

On Sunday morning, the four of us set off with an air of excitement. The journey was fairly straightforward. After stopping for lunch at a roadside cafe, we continued our journey, finally arriving outside a long row of terraced houses on a steep hill in the suburbs of Brighton, a little way back from the seafront.

A plump, middle-aged lady beamed at us when she opened the door and invited us inside. The house was small, and there were Colourpoint Persian cats everywhere I looked. They were sprawled on chairs, the table, window sill and worktops. Yet the house was immaculately clean with no odour of cats or litter trays, which reassured me that the cats were all well cared for.

In her back room, the lady handed me a small ball of fluff, which was the seal point boy I had come to see. My heart melted as he gazed up at me with round sapphire blue eyes that contrasted with his dark brown face.

"His pedigree name is Bobby Dazzler, the lady informed me.

"Oh, that's just what he is," I exclaimed, stroking his soft coat. I remembered to check that his bite was level. This was another detail that Debbie had shown me. Then, as he nuzzled against me, purring loudly, I knew I had found my future stud cat. Bobby Dazzler was the one.

The lady made us some tea, and we sat chatting and making a fuss of the cats. Mum and Dad were very taken with Bobby Dazzler. While we took turns cuddling him, the lady showed us photos of his dad, another handsome seal point, and gave me a couple of photos to keep.

She introduced us to Bobby's mum, a friendly, pretty blue Colourpoint. She showed me Bobby's vaccination card and pedigree, which was quite impressive, sprinkled with champions and the odd grand champion. She also assured me that her vet had confirmed he was entire, an essential requirement for a future stud cat.

As Bobby was old enough to leave, I settled him in the cat basket I had brought. After completing all the necessary paperwork, we said goodbye. I thanked the lady for letting me have her lovely seal point boy. Now, I just had to be patient for at least another year until Bobby matured into a handsome stud cat like his dad.

When I introduced him at home, Tia seemed indifferent to her future husband. Jojo was equally unimpressed with the scrap of fur that wanted to play with his tail. I was relieved there was no hostility, which reassured me they would all become friends, given time.

A lady came into the shop Wednesday morning and enquired whether I could board her cat while she was on holiday for two weeks. I said I would, as any extra income was welcome to help pay the bills.

The cat, a pretty, tabby and white female named Daisy, arrived in her basket. She seemed a little nervous, which was understandable given her new environment. I decided the back room of the shop wouldn't be suitable for her, fearing she might escape from there, as Linda and I were constantly in and out, tending to the caged animals. Instead, I took her home, ensuring she had a comfortable and safe space in my bedroom during her two-week stay.

All went well for the two weeks until the last day, and then disaster struck. The weather had turned from warm into a heatwave. My bedroom was hot and stuffy with all the windows closed. I took pity on Daisy, so in the morning, before I left for work, I opened a small top window a fraction to allow some fresh air into the room, making sure to secure the latch.

When I arrived home that evening, I discovered, to my dismay, that she had escaped. Somehow, she had managed to unlatch the window and squeeze out through the small opening.

I searched frantically for Daisy, calling her name, but there was no sign of her. I was devastated. How could I face her owners and tell them that I had lost their cat? They were due to collect her the following day.

Byron and I scoured the nearby streets and gardens, calling her, but all to no avail. Daisy was in an area she didn't know. I wondered where she would go. Would she try to make her way back home to Sidcup? I was aware that cats and dogs possessed incredible homing instincts. However, I fervently hoped Daisy wouldn't attempt such an arduous journey with so many dangerous, busy roads to cross.

I had the owners' address, so, hoping they were home from their holiday, the next morning, I decided to screw up my courage and face them at their house rather than wait for them to arrive at the shop. I knew I had to take responsibility for what had happened. I was determined to do everything I could to find Daisy.

As I stood on their doorstep, my heart pounded, and I felt sick inside. I could see the concern in their eyes as I explained what had happened, apologising profusely. The news shocked them, but they quickly took control of the situation.

"She might still be hiding somewhere near your home," the man said. "You must take us there immediately to search for her."

They jumped in their car and followed me as I drove home, desperately hoping their familiar voices might coax Daisy out of her hiding place if that was where she was.

We arrived at my bungalow, and they started searching my front and back gardens, calling Daisy's name, but without success. They extended their search along the cul-de-sac next to my bungalow, which backed onto the fenced-off overgrown grounds of the dairy. They called Daisy's name repeatedly.

Then, a miracle happened. Suddenly, Daisy emerged through the long grass in the grounds of the dairy and squeezed through the fence to greet her joyful owners. My relief was overwhelming, seeing her safe and well, reunited with her delighted owners. She didn't appear to be any the worse for her ordeal in the grounds of the dairy overnight. She must have heard me calling her the previous evening but had opted to remain hidden.

Her owners quickly put her in her basket and whisked her away with barely a word to me. They were understandably still very annoyed with me for losing their beloved cat, and I didn't blame them. I felt guilty for all the distress I had caused, so naturally, I couldn't ask for a boarding fee after such a disastrous stay for Daisy. I was just grateful that Daisy had been found.

The following Sunday, my parents again accompanied me and Byron to view more properties in Norfolk. We drove to the picturesque village of Pulham Market near the Suffolk border, where we had an appointment to see a house on the outskirts.

The house had extra rooms downstairs that had been converted into an annexe. This older property lacked kerb appeal when we first saw it with an unkempt driveway. The house needed a fresh coat of paint, and the metal Crittall windows showed signs of rust. The owners were a relatively young couple with several children.

They gave us a tour of their home, but the rooms seemed dingy and needed redecorating. We were unimpressed with the house, but a large outbuilding in the garden was used as a games room. It housed a full-size snooker table, which made Byron's eyes light up. Suddenly, he was keen for us to buy this property.

We thanked the owners for showing us around. Then we headed into the quaint village centre with its thatched cottages around the large village green.

We parked at the Falcon pub, where we had a delicious lunch and discussed the potential costs of renovating the house we had viewed. We were all in agreement that it failed to impress and required a lot of work, so in the end, we dismissed it as unsuitable.

After our disappointing viewing at Pulham Market, we set off for Attleborough. However, our journey was unexpectedly interrupted when we were flagged down by traffic police doing spot checks on vehicles.

I showed them my driving licence, but the tax disc on the windscreen caught their attention because it was out of date. With so many money problems at the shop, I had delayed getting my road tax renewed. Now, I would pay the price.

The police recorded my details and informed me of the impending fine. It was a crushing blow. The financial burden of the fine, especially amid the shop's money problems, was a bitter pill to swallow. My decision to delay paying the road tax had backfired, a lesson learned the hard way.

After my harrowing encounter with the police, we resumed our journey to Attleborough. Our destination was a magnificent, newly built, Georgian-style house. Despite being beyond our budget, I was thrilled at the prospect of seeing this grand property. The agents had encouraged us to view it, even if it was just to dream. But if we did decide we wanted it, we would need to make an offer well below the asking price.

The house, set in a quarter-acre plot, was a sight to behold, with its striking white pillars flanking the front door. It also had the advantage of an attached double garage but didn't have a separate annexe. However, I had carefully studied the layout in the brochure, and I was confident that the accommodation could be tailored to our needs. I could see Mum and Dad comfortably occupying the downstairs rooms while Byron and I made the most of the space upstairs.

We were greeted by a charming middle-aged couple who welcomed us into their spacious hall. At one end, a grand carved wooden staircase wound upstairs.

The rooms all opened off the hall, including a large kitchen, a dining room with access to the garage, a cloakroom, a snug that could be a comfortable lounge with patio doors leading out to the back garden and a double bedroom with an en suite bathroom. There was also a large utility room which we could all share.

Upstairs was equally spacious with a wide landing and all the rooms leading off it. There were two double bedrooms and a bathroom. At the far end, a door opened into an enormous lounge. A wall of windows with patio doors led into an enclosed balcony with far-reaching views across the fields. I could visualise this balcony as a dining area.

On the landing, next to the lounge, was a small drinks room with a sink for preparing and serving drinks through a serving hatch into the lounge. This room would easily convert into a small kitchen. I felt a small kitchen for me and Byron was a minor inconvenience we could live with in such a beautifully laid out house. Alternatively, we could convert the utility room downstairs into a second large kitchen. We felt this house had many exciting possibilities.

The owners had maintained this much-loved house in an immaculate condition. The lady produced professional aerial photos of the property to show us and also pictures of the property they hoped to buy. They made a point of emphasising that they could only accept the full asking price for their house in order to afford their next property.

Mum and Dad were visibly impressed with the space offered by the downstairs rooms. We all left the house feeling excited about the potential of this lovely home.

I fully understood the owners' situation and the need to secure their next property, so it seemed far too cheeky to make an offer on a property that appeared to be in pristine condition and worth every penny of the asking price, knowing the offer was likely to be rejected.

After a thorough discussion with my parents, we decided to continue our search for the perfect property. So, a fortnight later, we found ourselves back in Norfolk. Byron brought along his school chum, Ian, for company. They had been friends for many years. Ian had accompanied us on a holiday to Scotland with Joan and Cyril.

We arrived in the charming mid-Norfolk village of Gressenhall, nestled in the heart of the countryside. The village boasted a museum, a cosy pub, a bustling post office, and a picturesque large village green. Today, we had arranged to view some converted stables with two separate sets of accommodation.

Unfortunately, the stables, though well converted, were a let-down. The rooms were disappointingly small, and the part that would be Mum and Dad's rooms just wasn't big enough. The lack of reasonable garden space added to our disillusionment with the property. It starkly contrasted the spaciousness and potential of the house we had viewed at Attleborough.

We drove into East Dereham and enjoyed another Sunday roast at the Otters Holt in Church Street, as the food had been so good there the last time.

I was excited at the prospect of viewing the next property. On paper, it offered all the space we could possibly need, so I was eager to see if it would meet our expectations.

Rose Cottage had been vacant for a year, so we collected the keys from the agents' office in Dereham, on the corner of Church Street. We then headed towards the town of Fakenham and took the turning signposted to the village of Whissonsett, which led us along a single-track lane.

Arriving in the village High Street, we drove past the post office stores and the quaint mediaeval church with its bell tower, churchyard and an expanse of grass fronting it. Turning into London Street, we passed the village hall, and a village shop with a butcher's opposite. In front of us was an enormous horse chestnut tree overhanging the road. The tree stood in the grounds of Rose Cottage.

As we approached the grand entrance, we were immediately impressed. The ornately decorated, original gate flanked by pillars and curved brick and flint walls created a striking first impression. The long, sweeping drive leading to the cottage was a sight to behold. The brick and flint cottage sat well back inside its expansive walled grounds of well over half an acre.

The drive forked left to a detached two-storey annexe with a double garage. On the right of the drive stood a magnificent copper beech tree, pear and plum trees, and two sizeable mock orange blossom bushes.

On the left of the drive were four large rose beds set in a vast expanse of lawn, stretching across to a brick and flint wall.

I parked the car, and we climbed out in awe and disbelief at the sheer size and breathtaking beauty of the grounds. A second lawn to the rear of the property was dominated by a tall conifer near the rear wall, where I noticed a small wooden door tucked away in the corner.

Rose Cottage was a charming Georgian property with symmetrical sash windows on either side of the central front door, now hidden by a large porch built as a later addition. It blended seamlessly with its matching brick and flint walls. The solid, carved oak door was furnished with ornate black hinges and attractive metal studs, adding a touch of elegance to the entrance.

Byron and Ian eagerly ran off to explore the garden while I unlocked the front door and stepped into a generously sized lobby, which housed a cloakroom and toilet.

The original front door had been replaced by an internal glazed oak door leading into the hall. To the left, a dining room with dual-aspect windows looked out across the front garden. A relatively modern open fireplace had fitted shelving to one side with cupboards beneath and a serving hatch to the kitchen on the other side.

Across the hall was a large lounge. The 1920s tiled fireplace definitely wasn't to my taste. The far end of the lounge had a lower ceiling, hinting at the room's past as two separate spaces. I noticed that the windows in both rooms had wooden shutters with metal bars, adding a touch of character and security.

A door at the far end of the lounge opened into the kitchen, as did a door from the hall. The kitchen's low ceiling matched the ceiling height at the far end of the lounge. The kitchen was spacious, with ample room for a large dining table, and had a homely feel.

Polystyrene tiles adorned the ceiling, some falling off. The fitted units were pretty old, and some were missing. A recess, once a fireplace, housed an oil-fired boiler, and next to it, a long, padded bench seat offered ample room for a table, making a cosy dining area.

"There's some work to do here," I commented, gazing around.

Mum was busy inspecting a couple of large cupboards under the stairs. "But in the meantime, it's still habitable," she remarked. "I like the rustic tiled floor, and these two fitted cupboards are useful – a broom cupboard and a larder."

I could sense Mum's excitement as we explored the cottage. I knew we were thinking the same thing - this could be our new home.

Dad stayed in the lounge while Mum and I explored the bedrooms. Fortunately, the window sills were relatively low, so they made handy seats for Dad to sit on and get his breath back.

Upstairs, we discovered a half landing with two double bedrooms, a bathroom and a linen cupboard. Four more steps led to a top landing with two more double bedrooms and a single bedroom. The bedrooms were well-proportioned and offered plenty of natural light. The cottage exuded a sense of spaciousness, making it a comfortable and inviting space. Back downstairs, the kitchen door led into a covered passageway. At the end was a garden room with doors to a utility room and a storeroom. I discovered the missing kitchen units, which had been dismantled and stacked in the garden room.

A glazed door led outside to the rear garden, where I could see an old apple tree, blackcurrant bushes, and an overgrown vegetable patch with a beech hedge separating it from the rear lawn. The walled garden was a perfect spot for relaxation and outdoor activities.

Another door opened from the garden room into a massive greenhouse with well-established grape vines. The vines were trained on wires across the ceiling, so the bunches of red grapes hung down, making picking easy. The vines' roots were planted outside in root boxes where they could get sustenance from the rain.

"This looks like a typical Victorian setup," Dad remarked. He pointed to a large metal pipe that ran along one side of the greenhouse, below the windows. "That was used to heat the greenhouse. I expect the garden room once housed a boiler." The sight of the established grape vines further added to the nostalgic charm of the place.

Back along the passage, a back door led into an enclosed courtyard with a washing line, an oil tank for the central heating and a brick-built wood shed in the far corner.

"This place has so much to offer," I said, opening a side gate that led to the front driveway.

"Let's explore the annexe and check out its potential for Mum and me," Dad proposed eagerly.

I unlocked the front door of the more modern annexe and entered a hallway with a straight staircase leading to the upper floor. To the left, a compact dining room opened into a kitchen with a convenient walk-in pantry.

"I'm sure my dining table and chairs will fit in here," Mum said, sounding optimistic.

"And your cooker will fit in the kitchen," I added.

Dad sat on the stairs while Mum and I went upstairs to explore. A small landing had a bathroom on the left, complete with an airing cupboard and a spacious lounge on the right. A large picture window overlooked the driveway and beech tree with a view across to the church. A double bedroom was off the lounge with another picture window facing the beech tree.

"This lounge is so spacious, and the view is marvellous. There's plenty of room for our furniture in here," Mum declared excitedly as she gazed around, taking it all in. "The only problem is the stairs - your father wouldn't be able to manage them."

"We could easily install a chair lift, and then the upper floor will be readily accessible for Dad," I suggested. Mum smiled, looking relieved as she realised the problem had been resolved.

We drove home feeling excited about the possibilities that Rose Cottage offered. With its annexe and expansive grounds, this property was a more affordable option than the Georgian house at Attleborough, leaving us money to make any necessary improvements.

However, the task of finding buyers for our houses still loomed over us before we could fully embrace the potential of Rose Cottage.

September arrived, bringing threatening letters from the landlord's solicitors demanding payment for the shop's quarterly rent – money I simply did not have.

The stress and pressure this situation caused me was immense, and the worry of it all triggered the return of my gastric ulcer with a vengeance, a painful reminder that it had never gone away entirely. The pet shop sales continued to slump, compounding my worries.

Tucked away on a top shelf in the storeroom, I discovered a bundle of small wooden plant holders designed to hang on walls. I asked Linda about them, and she told me they were a job lot Anne had bought from a gypsy.

I decided we should do something with them, so I suggested to Linda that she plant the tubs with some of the small flowering plants we had and display them outside.

Linda had a flair for arranging the plants, using colours that blended well, so they soon attracted customers. The next day, as Linda was carrying some more tubs outside, she suddenly yelled. I hurried to the shop's door to see what the trouble was.

Linda was pointing along the road, looking angry. "That same gypsy was back with a friend, helping themselves to the tubs. I saw them run off, clutching several of them. I expect the gypsy recognised the planters and decided to steal some back."

I sighed. "That's all we need. Never mind, Linda, there's nothing we can do about it. Displaying goods outside is always a bit risky because we can't keep an eye on them all the time."

Still disgruntled about the stolen tubs, I was taken aback when a customer, noticing my tinned cat food prices, let out a disdainful snort.

"I can buy the same cat food along the road at Boots for a lot less than you are charging," she declared in a snooty voice. "Why do your tins of cat food cost more money?"

I glared at her. "Obviously, you'd be better off going to Boots for your cat food," I retorted. "Unlike me, Boots has the advantage of a long chain of shops, which gives them the buying clout to acquire their tins of cat food at a far cheaper price." The lady seemed to take offence at my curt reply. She simply turned and walked out without further comment.

"Another customer we've lost," I lamented to Linda, regretting my bad-tempered outburst. "This shop is getting me down."

"I think you need a cup of tea and a KitKat," Linda suggested with a smile, trying to cheer me up.

Mum and Dad invited Byron and me to Sunday lunch the following weekend. They had some exciting news they wanted to share with us.

Over dinner, they announced that they now had a buyer.

"A surveyor has been here, checking the house over," Mum said excitedly. "Yesterday, the agents rang to say a mortgage has been approved."

"That's fantastic news!" I exclaimed, feeling my spirits lifting. "What's your buyer like?"

"They are a young couple with a toddler. This will be their first proper home, so they are really keen to buy our house," Dad explained, looking pleased.

"Now, I just need to find a buyer for my bungalow, and I must also sell that flippin' shop before it bankrupts me," I declared, shaking my head.

"So you've had no luck as yet?" Mum enquired, seeing me looking down in the dumps.

I sighed. "No, but the agents have arranged a viewing of my bungalow for one evening next week."

"We'll keep our fingers crossed for you," Dad said with an encouraging smile.

"Once we both have our buyers in place, we'll be able to put an offer on Rose Cottage," Mum declared excitedly.

"Since it's been on the market for over a year, I don't suppose it'll get snapped up quickly," I surmised. I had been trying not to get my hopes up about Rose Cottage as we weren't in a position to make an offer on it yet, and the thought of losing it to another buyer was a constant worry.

Byron quietly ate his dinner, listening to us talking. Despite being intrigued by Rose Cottage and its grounds, he still had strong reservations about moving to Norfolk, where he would face the daunting prospect of attending a new secondary school, knowing no one. Trying to cheer him up, I promised him a snooker table once we had moved to Norfolk, recalling how thrilled he had been to

149

see the snooker table in the outbuilding at the house in Pulham Market.

On Wednesday evening, a well-dressed, discerning lady with a haughty manner arrived to view my bungalow. She had come from Sidcup and said she knew Flights Pet Shop when I mentioned that I owned it.

I didn't hold out much hope of her being interested in my bungalow because she found fault with nearly every room. Her criticisms felt like personal jabs, each chipping away at the emotional value I attached to my home.

In the lounge, she gazed around disdainfully. "I would prefer a larger lounge, so I'd have to knock down the adjoining wall to the front bedroom to create a spacious L-shaped room. And that fireplace would have to go," she added, giving an uninterested glance at my lovely Yorkstone fireplace that I had carefully installed with my brother's help.

The kitchen passed her scrutiny, except for the window. "I would change that for a bow window," she declared emphatically.

We moved into the adjacent unfinished extension. "If it wasn't for this extension, this bungalow wouldn't suit me at all," she remarked, walking around the new dining room and gazing through the patio doors to the back garden beyond. "It's a pity the sockets and switches aren't in place."

"The wiring is installed," I pointed out. "It's only the second fix for the electrics that's required."

After thoroughly inspecting all the rooms, she gave a dismissive sniff and decided she had seen enough. She left, expressing her intention to contact the agent.

Initially, I dismissed her as a time waster. However, to my utter amazement, a few days later, the agent contacted me with an unexpected offer from the lady of the full asking price. This surprising turn of events stunned and delighted me and succeeded in cheering me up.

Now, I just needed to get the shop sold. As the bank's reminders of the overdue loan payments became more relentless, I found myself in a desperate situation. I had no choice but to consider drastic measures. The pressure to sell the shop was mounting and tended to cloud my judgment.

I faced a moral dilemma. I knew potential buyers would want to see a thriving business, so I sat down at the weekend and made a second set of accounts for the shop. It was a painstaking process to present a more appealing picture of the business. These accounts showed the shop as a viable business with much better sales figures than the actual sales. It was a difficult decision, but I felt I had no option if I was ever to secure a buyer.

Now that both houses were considered as sold, subject to contract, I felt more confident about approaching the agents of Rose Cottage with an offer after first agreeing on the finances with my parents, as we would be going fifty-fifty on this new venture.

The asking price was £52,000, but I took into account the work needed and the fact that the cottage had been languishing on the market for over a year. I rang the agents and put in what I considered to be a reasonable offer of £47,000. Then, I waited on tenterhooks for my answer.

The agents, W.H. Brown of East Dereham, didn't keep me waiting very long. They rang me back at the shop with the good news that my offer had been accepted.

I explained my situation: Two houses were being sold in order to buy Rose Cottage, so the process could take a little longer than normal. The agents were incredibly understanding, assuring me it wouldn't be a problem since the cottage was vacant because the owners had already moved on.

I came off the phone feeling elated, and Linda was equally pleased for me. "This calls for a celebratory cup of tea and maybe two KitKats," she announced with a laugh.

My parents were over the moon when I rang to tell them the marvellous news. Our selling and buying procedures were now underway, except for the shop, which could put a spanner in the works. This thought was unsettling, but I was determined not to allow this setback to deter me from my goal.

As September drew to a close, there had been little interest in the shop and a dearth of potential buyers. Then, at the beginning of October, a call from the agents sparked a glimmer of hope - a lady was interested in a viewing.

She arrived late one afternoon when the shop was quieter than usual. I had instructed Linda on what to do while I was in the storeroom, showing the lady my accounts.

The pleasant, well-dressed middle-aged lady explained that she only wanted the shop for some pin money because she was bored being stuck at home while her husband was away on business.

After showing her around, I took her to my desk and produced my carefully doctored accounts for her to examine.

Meanwhile, I could hear Linda carrying out my instructions as she strode up and down the shop floor, opening and closing the door, causing the bell to jangle, followed by the sound of the till ringing. She was doing her best to create the illusion of a bustling business. I smiled, appreciating her efforts to deceive this lady into thinking she was considering a thriving enterprise.

Our efforts were all in vain because the lady never contacted the agents again. Her lack of interest was a disappointing blow, leaving me disillusioned and frustrated.

After a particularly boring day, with the driving rain keeping most shoppers at home, I closed the shop feeling fed up and keen to get home. The car's wipers struggled to clear the windscreen of the relentless downpour. The dark autumnal evening made the visibility even worse. I arrived at the junction where I joined the busy A road. It was rush hour, so there were unbroken streams of traffic in all three lanes, racing past in a hurry to reach their destinations. I felt trapped, waiting for a break in the traffic that didn't come. The headlights glared in the rain, making judging distances difficult. I began to despair of ever finding a break in the traffic.

After what felt like an age, I began to get frantic. No one was letting me out. In desperation, I decided to inch out in a last-ditch effort and hope that someone would let me into the inside lane. With my indicator blinking, I made my move – a big mistake!

Suddenly, a lorry was on top of me, blaring its horn. Panic-stricken, I stamped on the brake as the lorry roared past, missing my car by the merest fraction. I quickly reversed back and sat there, shaking, realising I had just had a very fortunate escape. How could I have been so stupid? It was a stark reminder of the importance of patience in such situations. My patience returned in abundance, and I waited until a long gap finally appeared in the streaming traffic. Only then did I pluck up the courage to pull out. I was thankful to reach home safely that evening, fully aware that it could have ended badly for me.

The following week, an unexpected visitor arrived at my pet shop. It was the owner of the tool hire shop located further along the parade. He introduced himself as Mark and said he had heard that my pet shop was for sale. He explained that he was considering expanding his tool hire business.

He already owned the DIY shop on the corner, next door to my shop. However, he made it clear that he would only be interested in buying my shop if the upstairs flat was vacant. At the moment, it was still occupied by the lady tenant whose regular weekly rent payments helped to bolster the flagging sales.

This unexpected visit and Mark's proposal brought a glimmer of hope, renewing my belief that I could sell the shop.

After Mark had left, Linda made some tea, and we tried but failed to come up with ideas for persuading the lady upstairs to vacate the flat. Pedro was perched on Linda's shoulder, his head cocked on one side as though listening to our conversation.

The doorbell jangled, announcing a customer. An elderly lady came in to buy some dog biscuits.

As she turned to leave, Pedro, in a mischievous mood, suddenly flew after her and landed with a loud squawk on her back. She bent over, terrified, trying to fend him off, then let out a scream and ran for the door with Pedro still clinging to her back.

Linda ran down the shop to retrieve the recalcitrant parrot. Fortunately, Pedro released his hold on the lady's coat and flew onto Linda's shoulder just as the lady reached the door.

She dashed outside in a panic, desperate to escape from what she considered to be a ferocious bird attacking her.

I shook my head in despair. "There goes yet another customer who will never set foot in this shop again."

Now that I had Bobby Dazzler, I decided to enter him in a cat show with Tia. I booked them into the Kentish Show being held at the Stour Centre in Ashford.

A week before the show, I bathed them both and then brushed their coats twice daily, sprinkled with talcum powder. When checking Bobby's ears, I noticed they weren't quite as clean as they should be, so I gave them an extra wipe with the cotton buds.

Early Saturday morning, Byron and I headed for Ashford, leaving Linda in charge of the shop once again. The sun was low in the sky, glaring through the windscreen, making driving a bit of a challenge. Tia and Bobby were fluffed and spruced in their baskets.

We joined the queue for vetting-in, but when our turn arrived, we were in for a shock. The vet examined Bobby's ears and concluded he couldn't pass him as he had discovered one or two ear mites. I was devastated. Still considering myself a novice, I hadn't paid sufficient attention to Bobby's ears.

I bundled Bobby back inside his basket and gave him to Byron with my car keys. I asked him to take Bobby back to the car. I became acutely aware of the curious looks from the other exhibitors in the queue. Much to my relief, Tia passed the vetting-in check, and I hurried into the main hall to settle her in her pen. I was fuming with Bobby's breeder, realising he must have had the ear mites when I brought him home. Still, I should have been more attentive and noticed the problem, even though Bobby's ears hadn't bothered him.

Once Tia was settled on her white blanket and received a final brush, I had to vacate the hall with the other exhibitors and kill time until the judges displayed the results around lunchtime. I joined Byron in the car, keeping Bobby company. I had brought a flask of coffee and snacks for us to enjoy as we waited for the results.

The day turned out to be a disappointing one as Tia didn't win her open class. Several cats were in her class, and another lovely Colourpoint girl came first. I chatted to the owner who introduced herself as Anne Bailey. She told me she was also showing a couple of beautiful Chinchillas who had won their classes.

We packed up at the end of the day, feeling a little disheartened and keen to return home. Tia had a few more rosettes but no challenge certificate. I would have to get some treatment for Bobby's ears quickly, as I didn't want the problem spreading to Tia or Jojo.

Chapter Eight

A Sad Farewell

At the beginning of November, I received an excited phone call from Joan. Stella had given birth to a healthy baby boy on the second of November after her successful attempt at the artificial insemination program.

She had named him Stewart, after her brother, Stuart, only spelling the name differently. I was overjoyed to hear this news and couldn't wait to meet little Stewart.

Joan went on to tell me all about the birth. "Poor Stella suffered a horrendous time. She had to have a caesarian, but the anaesthetic didn't work properly. She remained conscious all the way through the delivery, but the anaesthetic left her paralysed, so she couldn't speak or move to alert the nurses to the agonising pain she was suffering."

"Oh, that sounds like a real nightmare!" I gasped in shock. "I can't even begin to imagine how difficult that must have been for Stella. I've never heard of that happening."

"She was very traumatised, but I'm sure she'll get over it now she's got the baby she so desperately wanted. Mick will continue working in Saudi Arabia while Stella stays home, caring for their baby. I daresay he'll be looking for work in the UK to be at home with his family."

We caught up on our other news. Joan was concerned to hear that the pet shop wasn't working out as I had hoped. I reassured her I had a plan and felt optimistic about the future. She was thrilled that we intended to move to Norfolk once our houses and the shop were sold.

"We find the supermarket hard work, even with the staff we employ to help us," Joan admitted. "But we do love living in Norfolk, and I'm sure you will, too. We'll be able to see a lot more of you and Byron once you've moved."

The day after Stewart was born, Dad celebrated his 74th birthday. Despite his insistence that he didn't want any fuss, Byron and I joined Dad and Mum for dinner at their house that evening for a modest celebration.

I was suffering from a painful back after putting it out while struggling to carry a large sack of peanuts into the shop. This was a long-standing, recurring injury caused originally when Byron was a toddler. I tried to uproot a three-foot-tall obstinate weed, tugging hard at it, but the weed won when my back gave out and left me in agony for several weeks. Ever since, I have had to be careful when bending or lifting anything. However, after a few months with no back pain, I tend to forget until I lift something I shouldn't, and then the searing pain returns with a vengeance.

A few weeks later, Mum rang me to say that Dad had been admitted to hospital for his usual treatment after a particularly bad bout of breathlessness. "He's been telling the nurses about the bungalow he will be moving to in Norfolk."

"What bungalow?" I asked, puzzled.

Mum laughed. "Oh, he gets a bit confused and forgetful these days. He really means Rose Cottage."

I promised Mum I'd accompany her on Sunday afternoon to visit Dad.

157

When I arrived at the hospital with Mum, I was shocked to enter the ward and see Dad sitting on a chair in the middle of the ward, huddled up in a blanket, watching the entrance as he waited impatiently for our arrival. He looked much older and frailer than when I visited him on his birthday. To make matters worse, he now had a bloodshot eye.

We walked Dad back to his bed, and while we chatted, I trimmed his toenails. Dad, who had always loved his food, complained about the poor quality of the hospital food, so Mum promised to make him his favourite dish, steak and kidney pudding, and bring it in the next day.

When we left the hospital at the end of visiting time, Dad seemed much more cheerful, looking forward to a tasty meal during Mum's visit on Monday.

At 5 a.m. the next morning, Mum received an urgent phone call from the hospital, asking her to visit Dad immediately. The sudden change in Dad's condition filled her with concern as she hurried there, fearing the worst.

She arrived on his ward to see curtains drawn around his bed. There was no familiar cough, only silence. In that moment, Mum realised she had lost her husband. Dad had died minutes before she reached his bedside.

Mum returned home and rang to tell me the sad news. "I gave him a kiss goodbye - he looked very peaceful, as though he was just sleeping." She sounded strangely detached and unemotional, as though Dad's death hadn't properly registered with her.

I broke the news gently to Byron over breakfast. He was saddened, but with Dad's health in decline for some time, it wasn't totally unexpected. Byron put on a brave face and insisted he would be fine going to school. After he had left, I drove to Mum's house to see how she was coping. Like Mum, I was feeling emotionally numb, unable to react to the loss of my wonderful dad.

I noticed the larder door ajar as I walked in the back door. There on a shelf was a solitary individual steak and kidney pudding. Mum had made it ready to take to the hospital. A great sadness swept through me as I realised Dad never got to enjoy his favourite dish one last time.

I found Mum sitting at the dining room table, sorting through a bundle of papers. "There's a mountain of official paperwork to get organised," she complained.

"There's no need to do it straight away. I'm sure Roger and me can help you with it," I said, trying to ease her anxiety.

"I feel better if I'm keeping busy," Mum said. "The sale of this house might be delayed because your dad and I both needed to sign the contracts. Now, the house will have to be altered into my sole name."

"Don't worry about that. The solicitor can reorganise everything in due time. After all, I haven't found a buyer for the shop yet." I tried to sound upbeat about the work ahead of us.

Roger suddenly appeared at the lounge door, looking sombre. We hadn't heard him come in. "After your phone call early this morning, Mum, I thought I'd better pop round and check on you," he said.

"Oh, I'm fine," Mum said dismissively. I left them talking and went to the kitchen to make some coffee. When I returned, Roger was telling Mum about a short dream he had before he was awakened by her phone call telling him that Dad had died.

"This dream was strange and really vivid. It stayed with me when I woke up instead of fading away, as dreams usually do. In this dream, Dad came to see me and told me he wanted to say goodbye because he was leaving, but Dad didn't say where he was going. I woke up feeling puzzled, but after your phone call, suddenly, it seemed to make sense – Dad was saying his final goodbye to me!"

I smiled, handing him a coffee. "That's a really nice dream to have at such a sad time."

Roger nodded. "Yes, I shan't forget that dream easily."

159

I left Roger helping Mum arrange the papers in order of urgency, spreading them out on the table.

Like Mum, I needed to keep busy, so I headed for work, hoping the shop would help me through this difficult time. In the shop, I explained what had happened to Linda. She gasped in surprise. "Oh, Ann, I'm so sorry. You shouldn't have come into work today – you're in no fit state to serve customers."

I started to protest, insisting that I was fine, when quite unexpectedly, my emotions burst out, releasing a flood of tears. Linda hugged me and implored me to go home and not return until I felt better.

"You have no need to worry about the shop. I can look after it fine on my own," she assured me.

I was taken aback by how vulnerable I felt now that I had given way to my pent-up emotions. Instead of arguing with Linda, I simply nodded and left to return home.

Dad's death sent me into a state of deep depression. Nevertheless, I managed to help Mum with the arrangements for the funeral service. We had a lot of people to notify, so while I was occupied doing this, I left Linda in charge at the shop.

Then, early one morning, before I awoke, like Roger, I had a vivid dream about Dad that stayed with me after waking up. It seemed so real, uplifting my spirits and easing my troubled mind. The dream was a turning point in my grieving process. It felt like Dad had come to me to say his final goodbye, and it gave me the strength to accept his passing and move forward.

In my dream, I found myself at a party in a house I couldn't place. Dad was casually leaning against an ornate, white mantelpiece, his Mac and bow tie as familiar as ever. (For the last few years, Dad had taken to wearing a bow tie.) I was seated on a sofa, and he came and sat beside me. As Dad held my hand, I was surprised by the warmth. I had anticipated his hand to be cold since he was no longer with us.

160

"You don't need to worry about me anymore," Dad reassured me with a smile. "I'm alright because I'm with God now."

Dad had never been a religious man. He never attended church except for the occasional wedding, christening or funeral. This made his words in my dream all the more surprising. Though unexpected, his words brought a sense of peace and comfort that stayed with me long after I awoke. It was as if a great weight had been lifted off me. I felt happier, knowing that Dad had moved on to a better place. The dream gave me the closure I needed. I was sure he would have appreciated knowing that he had died during the same year as his two favourite comedians, Tommy Cooper and Eric Morecambe, so he was in good company.

Dad's funeral was held on the 4th of December. The sedate hearse drew up beside the green, opposite the house where Dad had lived for the last thirty-five years.

Mum, Roger, Byron and I followed the hearse in an immaculate black limousine. We were each lost in our thoughts, the weight of the day heavy on our shoulders. We were united in our shared grief.

All I could visualise was Dad lying in his coffin, still sporting a bloodshot eye. I pushed the image from my mind by thinking back to happier times when Dad's zany humour often received a reprimand from Mum.

I remembered our card games dissolving into laughter when Dad displayed the card everyone else wanted, stuck to his bald patch while gurning with a toothless grin. Dad had passed on his love of card games to me over the years.

Then I pictured the Shrove Tuesday fiasco when he hit a pancake for six, causing it to stick to the ceiling. It hung there for a week before Dad could be persuaded to scrape it off, leaving a greasy mark to tell the tale.

So many moments with Dad were filled with joy and laughter, like when my friend Christine came for tea. A large jelly took pride of place in the centre of the table.

With his mischievous sense of humour, while Mum was out of the room, Dad couldn't resist smacking a serving spoon onto the jelly, causing it to splatter, giving everyone an unwanted helping in the hair and face. We couldn't help laughing, even if it was at our own expense.

I smiled to myself as I reminisced about the countless times when, as a young child, Dad's jokes would send me into fits of uncontrollable laughter, causing me to wet my knickers, much to Mum's annoyance.

My mind wandered back to our exciting trips to Margate on his motorbike at the end of his stint of night shifts. In the autumn, we would stop on the side of the Thanet Way to pick blackberries.

At Margate, Dad would take a peaceful nap on a bench while I played on the beach, collecting seashells and mussels. These heart-warming moments remain vivid in my memory, defining our close relationship.

Dad's role as an ambulance driver was not just a job but a treasure trove of humorous anecdotes. One of his stories that made me smile was when he was asked to recover a mental patient who had wandered off on Dartford Heath dressed as a Martian with a colander on his head, complete with antennae. These stories, told with Dad's own brand of humour, are etched in my memory.

Dad's influence extended beyond his job. He had even taught my teacher at junior school how to drive a St. John's ambulance.

But perhaps his most significant role was when he stepped in as a surrogate father to my friend, Katy Bullinaire, and her younger brother, Colin, after they lost their dad to leukaemia at a young age. Dad's caring nature helped them to cope with life's difficult times. His absence would be an enduring loss.

I recalled Dad's recent phone call, asking me to visit him. It sounded urgent, so I dropped everything and dashed over to his house. But when I arrived, there was nothing specific that Dad wanted; he just needed to see me. This was a touching moment, uncharacteristic of him, as if he had a premonition that his time was running out.

All these cherished memories came flooding back to me as I stared at the coffin travelling in front of me to the crematorium.

The ceremony went smoothly, and afterwards, we gathered around the flowers and wreaths displayed on the lawn outside, each bearing poignant messages of love and loss.

I felt sad because I had to settle for a modest wreath of yellow roses, a compromise dictated by my financial constraints. I could only hope that Dad, having been thrifty all his life, would understand my situation.

Mum arranged for Dad's ashes to be kept by the undertakers and then forwarded to the local vicar once we had moved to Rose Cottage. She planned to purchase a plot in the churchyard and have Dad's ashes buried in their joint grave.

Mum's youngest sister, my Auntie Con, travelled by train from St Annes-on-Sea near Blackpool to keep Mum company for a week, now that she had to adapt to living independently.

Mum decided there would be no decorations in the house this Christmas. Putting up the decorations and balloons had always been Dad's job. In her present state of bereavement, as far as she was concerned, Christmas had been cancelled.

I was back working in the shop and pleased to see that sales were improving slightly now that we stocked Christmas goodies for customers to buy for their pampered pooches and pussies. This improvement in sales was a small comfort during a difficult time.

The lady who owned Daffy Duck called in at the shop with a heavy heart. She told us the distressing news of Daffy's disappearance. She looked very worried as she expressed her fear that Daffy might end up as someone's Christmas dinner.

"The children are devastated. I don't think we'll have any success finding Daffy again," she said with a sigh.

My heart went out to the lady. Daffy was not just a pet but a cherished member of their family, a character who had left an indelible mark on their lives.

I popped round to Mum's one evening to visit my Auntie Con while she was staying there. I was surprised to find Mrs Bullinaire also visiting Mum.

Mum sat quietly, listening to Con and Mrs Bullinaire chattering non-stop. Perhaps this was their way of distracting Mum from sad thoughts of Dad. She couldn't have got a word in, even if she had wanted to!

Mrs Bullinaire had always been able to talk the hind leg off a donkey, but now she had serious competition from Con. I got the impression that each was trying to out-talk the other. Meanwhile, Mum sat in her chair, and I could tell from the odd glance she gave me that she was just wishing for some peace and quiet. I decided not to stay too long as Mum already had more company than she really wanted.

With Christmas fast approaching, Byron and I agreed to take his unwanted toys to a local boot sale at Dartford football ground. Byron had many toys he had long outgrown, so he helped me choose which ones he no longer wanted. Early Sunday morning, I loaded them into the Escort and drove the short distance to the football ground.

We carefully arranged the toys and games on our stall and soon parents and children were drawn to the colourful array of items. We were kept busy doing a brisk trade.

Suddenly, the heavens opened, and the rain came down in torrents. Like everyone else, we quickly gathered up our things and dashed to the shelter of the covered terraces, where we continued to ply our trade until the toys were all sold.

We came home pleased with our day's work and with some extra money towards the expenses incurred by Christmas.

We spent a quiet Christmas at home, inviting Mum to join us for dinner as it was her first Christmas without Dad.

After dinner, we opened presents and then relaxed, watching the ITV comedy feature film, 'Return of the Pink Panther.'

I re-opened the shop the day after Boxing Day. I was delighted to receive an unexpected Christmas present from the lady renting the upstairs flat when she came into the shop and handed in her notice. This was a surprising but very welcome gift. She explained that she and her boyfriend were buying a place together.

With the flat about to become vacant, I couldn't wait to tell Mark, the owner of the tool hire shop, the good news. He had told me that he would only consider purchasing the pet shop if the flat above it was vacant. I kept my fingers crossed, hoping this was still the case, as I hurried along the parade to his shop.

I entered his large, bright shop, immaculately fitted out with every tool imaginable. Mark looked pleased to see me. I felt greatly relieved when he assured me he was still interested in buying the shop. He added that he would even consider keeping it as a pet shop.

"I had intended extending my tool hire business," he explained. "But if your accounts show the business is viable, then I'll continue to sell pet supplies."

I felt guilty as I handed him the second set of doctored accounts. A few days later, Mark returned them with a smile.

"They look fine," he declared. "I have no worries about continuing in the same line of business. However, if, for any reason, it doesn't work out, then I can always revert back to my original plan and sell tools instead."

Mark's words eased my conscience, knowing he had the wherewithal to sell alternative goods when he discovered the pet trade wasn't as good as the accounts portrayed.

He was keen to keep Pedro as a pet for his son. "He'll be over the moon, having his very own talking parrot," Mark told me excitedly. I didn't mention that Pedro harboured a deep aversion to men. I had grave misgivings about his son and Pedro getting along. It was a bittersweet moment, knowing that Pedro would have a new home but also worrying about his future.

We soon instructed solicitors to proceed with the legalities of selling and buying the shop. I was pleased there were no estate agent fees, as they hadn't supplied the buyer.

I felt as if a great weight had been lifted off my shoulders. I tried not to get my hopes up about owning Rose Cottage. There was quite a way to go with the legal paperwork, and things could still go wrong.

The new year of 1985 arrived, and I was pleased and relieved to be leaving 1984, my annus horribilis. Looking back, it had been the worst year of my life. As the new year dawned, I was hopeful for better times ahead, feeling excited for the possibilities it held.

On January 1st, mobile phone calls were made for the first time, making this a landmark groundbreaking event.

One day, while perusing the local paper during my lunch break, I stumbled upon a part-time job opportunity in Sidcup. It caught my interest as it could provide some much-needed extra money. I talked it over with Linda, and she agreed to manage the shop on her own for a few hours each afternoon if I were to secure the position.

The job was at a car showroom in Sidcup High Street. I made the call and was promptly invited for an interview.

The work was familiar, involving office tasks I had mastered over the years. The only potential hurdle was using a microfiche reader, a device I had never encountered. However, the manager's reassurance that it wouldn't be a problem put my mind at ease.

The manager was eager for me to start as soon as possible, so I arranged to begin work the following afternoon. I was confident Linda could manage the shop alone for the few hours I would be at the showroom.

Working in the office at the car showroom made a refreshing change and gave me a brief respite from the worries at the pet shop. I had my own small office adjacent to the manager's. He patiently guided me through the microfiche system, which I found surprisingly user-friendly.

As the weather turned colder, with frequent snow showers, the manager, a spirited young man in his early thirties, revealed his love for driving in the snow. His eyes lit up as he described the thrill of racing through the snow and executing a perfect spin using the handbrake. His passion was evident, and I couldn't help smiling at his enthusiasm, even if it wasn't my idea of fun!

On January 10th, the Sinclair C5 was launched. This battery assisted recumbent tricycle was considered to be a fun machine by many people.

By January 13th, the temperatures had plummeted further, and a substantial six inches of snow blanketed the area, making driving a daunting task.

I arrived home late one evening the following week. As I stepped out of the car, I could hear the worrying sound of running water. The weather had warmed up slightly, causing a thaw.

I hurried into my back garden, trying to locate the source of the running water. I looked across at my neighbour's house and was horrified to see water gushing out of the bedroom windows and cascading down the walls. Where it had refrozen, thick layers of ice had formed.

My neighbour, Miss Smart, was an elderly spinster who had lived there alone since the house was built in the

1930s. She had been living downstairs for many years, as she could no longer manage the stairs. I dashed to her front door and rang her doorbell, but there was no answer. The situation was becoming increasingly worrying.

I hurried to the next house and knocked on their door. A lady answered and told me Miss Smart was away, staying with some friends. I was relieved to hear that she was safe.

"I believe she may have left a key with the people living opposite," the lady told me.

I thanked her and ran across the road to the house opposite. The lady living there confirmed that she did have a key. I explained that Miss Smart's pipes had burst and the water must be turned off. She was quick to offer her help.

"I'll send my husband over there to turn off the main stop cock. Then I'll ring the emergency services and get someone to clear up the mess and dry out the house. Miss Smart won't be able to return there to live until it's thoroughly dry again." The woman seemed very competent, so I left her to make all the necessary arrangements.

I received a worrying phone call at the shop from the agent, W.H. Brown, who was selling Rose Cottage. The agent informed me that someone else also wanted to buy Rose Cottage. He then went on to make what I considered to be an underhanded proposition. As the purchase was taking so long, he suggested we have a race for contracts to hurry things along. I was shocked by the agent's lack of integrity. The unexpectedness of his dodgy-sounding proposal left me reeling. With two houses and a shop to sell, I couldn't hurry. With a heavy heart, I told the agent the other interested party could have Rose Cottage, then hung up.

I was devastated at losing Rose Cottage and disgusted with the agent for even suggesting a race for contracts. I had no choice because I didn't want to enter a race I would almost certainly lose. The agent's betrayal left me feeling deeply disappointed and disillusioned.

Later that day, the agent rang me back to say the situation had changed. I could now buy Rose Cottage, and it was no longer necessary to have a race for contracts. The other potential buyer had fizzled away. I strongly suspected there never was another buyer. The agent was simply getting impatient to sell Rose Cottage, which had been languishing on their books for a long time.

I was relieved that the purchase of Rose Cottage could proceed, taking all the time necessary for the solicitors to carry out their work. However, I couldn't shake off the feeling of wariness towards the agent, who I felt could no longer be trusted due to his pushy tactics.

My mother and I initially decided to forgo a property survey to save on moving costs. However, as Rose Cottage was a Georgian property, there could be some issues that needed addressing, so I had a change of heart and asked Roger if he would check out the cottage and give it his seal of approval. As a qualified carpenter and window fitter, he had some experience in the building trade. He had an idea of what problems to look for in an older property.

He was glad to be of help and looked forward to spending the weekend in Norfolk with Shelley, doing a survey of the property. He was also curious to see the cottage that had won our hearts and lured us away from Kent. In return for his help, I paid for him and Shelley to stay at the Otters Holt Hotel in East Dereham on Saturday night.

My main concern was an obvious crack and bulge in the flint wall on the corner of the property beside the dining room window. I had noticed this crack when we first viewed the cottage, and it was a potential indicator of structural problems that could be costly to repair.

Roger called in Monday evening to give me his assessment of the survey he had conducted. We sat in the kitchen, drinking coffee, and he produced a notebook.

"I jotted down some notes while I was checking out the cottage. Overall, I couldn't find anything seriously wrong. I don't think that crack in the wall is an urgent problem, although it might need attention in the future. I had a good look around the loft, and you'll be pleased to know the rafters are all new. I found a few Norfolk reeds that had once been on the roof when it was thatched. I suspect the thatch caught fire, and the roof had to be replaced – hence, the new rafters beneath a pantiled roof. I couldn't find any sign of a damp course, so that may be a job you will want to do. The window sills are all solid oak and will last forever without rotting."

I was pleased that Roger had been so thorough. His assessment put my mind at ease and would reassure our mother. This was Mum's first real experience of buying a property, and there was always a slight worry, especially when purchasing an older property. We now felt confident that Rose Cottage was a sound investment.

Towards the end of January, Miss Smart's house had finally been dried out, using industrial dryers upstairs and downstairs, running twenty-four hours a day. As I was leaving for work one morning, I saw the lady from across the road who had organised everything. She was coming out of her front gate, so I went over to ask her if there was any news. She informed me that Miss Smart would not be returning to her house.

"She's living in a care home now, and once the water damage in her house has been repaired, the house will be put on the market."

Miss Smart, Byron, Mum, and I were embarking on new lives elsewhere or about to embark on them. When I first moved to the bungalow, Miss Smart had been a frequent visitor, using her two walking sticks as she wasn't very mobile. I recalled Byron and me having great difficulty extracting her from my armchair when it was time for her to leave. Byron would push her from behind while I tugged her arms. Only after she had uncrossed her feet did we have any success!

On one occasion, she asked me to give her a lift to the Co-op in town so she could buy a new corset. That trip became an embarrassing fiasco when she deliberately left her old, stained corset hidden under a chair in the changing room. An assistant discovered it and chased after us through the throng of shoppers, waving the stained corset at me and yelling, "I think you forgot this." She handed it to me, and I quickly stuffed it in my bag, wishing the floor would swallow me up. Meanwhile, Miss Smart had walked on, oblivious to my awkward predicament.

At the end of January, the much-anticipated completion date for the shop finally arrived. This had been achieved far quicker than when I purchased the shop. The news came as a tremendous relief, knowing that the shop would be off my hands in just two more weeks. It was a liberating moment and a significant step towards achieving my new life in Norfolk.

With the upstairs flat now vacant, I decided to order a load of books to be delivered to the flat, knowing I would be long gone before the book company came looking for payment. Although unethical, I considered it a small repayment for the thousands of pounds I had lost the previous year while managing the shop.

Mark, the new owner, had agreed to keep Linda on, recognising her expertise in the pet trade. Linda was delighted and relieved to hear this. She had feared losing her job once the shop was sold, but now she could rest assured, knowing her job was secure. I was glad that Linda could continue doing the work she loved.

A week later, I handed in my notice at the car showroom. The work had been easy but also rather monotonous. I was eagerly looking forward to starting a new chapter in my life, so I didn't feel any regrets about leaving the following week.

Byron accompanied me to work on my last day at the shop as it was a Saturday, and there was stocktaking to do.

Before we started work on the stocktaking, I loaded the car with anything I might need for the cats: baskets, litter trays, food dishes and beds. The day was filled with conflicting emotions. I was glad to be finally rid of the shop, which had a mixture of good and bad memories, but I felt sad to be leaving Linda.

As I prepared to depart, she surprised me with a thoughtful gift - a cement garden ornament of a Persian cat, knowing I planned to breed Colourpoint Persians once I had moved to Norfolk. I found her gesture very touching.

She also gave me three plaster of Paris wall plaques of horses' heads that she had painstakingly made and painted. I thanked her, but I could see Byron pulling a face at them behind Linda's back. He clearly wasn't impressed by her handiwork.

As I left, I gave Linda a hug and promised to visit her once she was running the shop for Mark, the new owner.

I drove home feeling elated as the burden of the shop, a constant source of stress and financial strain, had finally been lifted off my shoulders.

Byron and I celebrated this new-found freedom with a meal from our favourite Chinese takeaway. At last, I was free from the shop, which had become such a millstone around my neck. The bank's threatening letters would still drop through my letterbox until my bungalow was sold. However, the sale of the shop marked a significant step towards financial freedom.

With the luxury of free time, I eagerly planned a visit to Rose Cottage with Mum and Byron. Our aim was to do some measuring in preparation for the day when we could make our permanent move to the tranquil Norfolk countryside, leaving the stresses of Kent far behind. The prospect of a peaceful life in a quiet Norfolk village filled

Mum and me with hope and excitement, though not Byron, who was still unenthusiastic.

I put together a picnic to take with us, and we set off on a bright, crisp Saturday morning. I stopped off in East Dereham to collect the keys from the agents before driving to the quiet, rural village of Whissonsett, accessed by a single lane with the occasional pull-in place for passing. The serene surroundings immediately put me at ease. After all the worry of the pet shop, I was eager to start a stress-free life in this rural idyll.

As I turned in at the open gate of Rose Cottage, the irritating sight of children's bikes scattered on the driveway shattered my rose-tinted glasses.

I stopped by the front door and walked around the corner to the greenhouse, where I discovered several local children inside, enjoying their own picnic. I was surprised to find the greenhouse door unlocked.

Their presence annoyed me – it felt like an intrusion on what was supposed to be a peaceful visit to our future home. I ordered them out and told them they were trespassing.

They gathered their things together, mumbled an apology, and then quickly jumped on their bikes and rode off down the drive.

Looking around the greenhouse, I couldn't see any fresh damage. There were broken panes, but they had been broken for some time. I checked that the door to the garden room was locked. I felt relieved that at least the children hadn't been able to gain access to the house.

"I shall report this to the agents when I return the keys and complain about the greenhouse door being left unlocked," I said as I unlocked the front door and we trooped through to the lounge.

Despite the chilly February weather, the cottage felt warm and cosy, its thick, lined walls providing sound insulation. The heating was turned on low to keep the place aired and dry while it stood empty and also to prevent the pipes from freezing.

We carefully measured for the curtains and worked out where the furniture would fit best. Then, we checked out the annexe. Everything looked the same as when we were there in the summer.

Mum paused at the lounge window, her eyes drawn to the breathtaking carpet of crocuses, snowdrops, and winter aconites spread beneath the copper beech tree. "Just look at that gorgeous expanse of flowers!" she exclaimed, her voice filled with wonder. "I've never seen so many." I joined her, and we both marvelled at the stunning display.

Back in the cottage, Byron and I sat on the lounge carpet while Mum perched on the window sill as we enjoyed our picnic. Then Mum made a surprising announcement.

"Now that Dad is no longer with us, I've been thinking. I'm not keen on the idea of living on my own in the annexe. This cottage has plenty of space to accommodate all of us comfortably as it's got five bedrooms."

Mum's unexpected decision to move into Rose Cottage with Byron and me caught us completely off guard. I assured her it wouldn't be a problem, but I couldn't shake off my reservations.

Our relationship when I was a teenager living at home had always been tense. We often fell out, and eventually, I left to live in a bedsit in London. However, I've matured since then, and I'm hopeful this new living arrangement will work out. Nevertheless, I can't help but feel a little apprehensive, worried that our past conflicts might resurface and we would find living together again a strain on our relationship. Still, I'm optimistic we can overcome them and make this work.

I tried to concentrate on the positive aspects of sharing a house with Mum: the potential of teamwork in sharing the housework and the bills. Also, I could get her to make the pastry, as I regarded hers as far superior to mine.

Another thought occurred to me. "If you intend to live in Rose Cottage, then we could consider letting out the annexe. It would be a good way to earn some extra income."

Mum perked up. "That sounds like a practical solution. I think short holiday lets would be ideal."

"We'll have to look into that possibility once we've settled in," I said, packing away our things, ready to head home.

We dropped off the keys at the agent's office on our way, and I mentioned the children trespassing on the property. The agent promised to inform the owner and ensure that the greenhouse door was kept locked.

Spring had finally arrived, and a week later, I visited Linda at the pet shop to see how she was coping.

I walked into a very different shop from the one I had left last month. I was greeted by silence. No birds were chirping, screeching or singing. There were no longer sacks of corn standing on the floor.

The gardening section had gone to be replaced by new, sleek, modern stands holding various products, from designer dog coats to expensive collars and leads, plus many more accessories. Cages and pens in an assortment of sizes were displayed where the fish tanks had once stood.

All the pet food was pre-packed and stacked on shelves. The scales for weighing the loose biscuits, peanuts and corn were gone, as were the large bins. There were no longer any animals or birds; in fact no livestock at all.

Linda stood behind the counter looking bored, wearing a smart new overall. She beamed with delight when she saw me enter.

"Wow! This place has changed!" I exclaimed in surprise.

"Yes, it certainly has," Linda said, her voice tinged with a hint of bitterness as she gave me a warm hug. "There's much less to do now everything is pre-packed in handy bags. I miss having the animals to care for, and, of course, there's no Pedro."

Now the shop was no longer mine, I refused Linda's offer of a cup of tea in case it might get her into trouble.

"How is Mark's son getting along with Pedro?"

Linda's face lit up. "Would you believe it! They have become the best of friends – inseparable!"

"Well, I never thought that would happen," I said, surprised by this good news. "And how is the business doing?"

"Not as well as Mark had hoped. As you can see, he's stocked up with loads of pet accessories displayed on posh new stands, but I think the shop has a sterile feel about it now. It lacks the character it had before."

I gazed around the shop, now neat and orderly, and had to agree with Linda. I couldn't help but feel a pang of nostalgia for the welcoming bird song. The screeching cockatiels and Pedro's noisy chatter were no more than a memory. The familiar aroma of the loose feeds, hay, and straw was gone.

"Mark is disappointed that the turnover isn't better, so he's still assessing whether to continue to run the shop as a pet shop."

"He'll struggle, as I did, having to compete with the pet shop in the High Street," I said. "They are determined to get rid of any competitor."

Linda sighed. "Yes, you're right. I daresay Mark will eventually give up; after all, this isn't a business he's really interested in running. If the turnover doesn't improve significantly, then I expect he'll convert it into another tool shop."

As I was leaving, I asked Linda to keep me informed of any changes at the shop, as she had my home phone number.

I had reached another crucial crossroads in my life. My thoughts were turning to my future at Rose Cottage and a new venture, breeding Colourpoint Persians.

All my aspirations currently rested on my lovely Tia Maria and Bobby Dazzler. I was determined to make this project a success, but I realised that if I was going to achieve an income from breeding Persians, I would need more cats.

After careful consideration, I decided to invest in a female Chinchilla kitten. I had studied them at the Kentish Cat Show. Their beauty was undeniable; their lightly ticked white coats gave them a shimmering silvery look, and their gorgeous green eyes were captivating. Chinchillas became very popular after appearing in the Kosset Carpet adverts, significantly increasing their demand and value in the market.

I decided to contact Anne Bailey. After our conversation at the Kentish Show, her cats had left a strong impression on me. I rang her and was thrilled to learn she had a kitten suitable for breeding. I immediately arranged a visit for the next day.

Anne greeted me warmly when I arrived at the mid-terraced house in Gravesend. As I entered the hall, I was welcomed by several Chinchilla cats and also a few Colourpoint Persians. She told me she owned a number of Chinchillas and had now included Colourpoint Persians in her breeding cattery.

Anne ushered me into her lounge and brought in a gorgeous, fluffy Chinchilla kitten, approximately six months old.

"I bred her and intended to keep her," Anne explained. "But, unfortunately, she has now received a scratch on one eye, so she is no longer suitable to show. My vet examined her and assured me the scratch didn't affect her sight. However, a judge at a show would mark her down. Therefore, I've decided to part with her."

I cuddled the pretty little kitten, stroking her soft coat. She gazed up at me with a slightly drunken look caused by her scratched eye, which was a little glazed.

"Of course, she is still eminently suitable for breeding," Anne added, "and she has a good pedigree."

As I held her in my arms, she purred loudly. The scratched eye didn't worry me. I agreed to buy her without any hesitation. The kitten hadn't yet been registered, so I could choose her pedigree name. I decided to call her Crystal as it suited her.

Once we had completed the paperwork, Anne was keen to show me the latest boy she had bred and kept to show. She brought in a magnificent, chunky kitten dripping with really long fur. He was even more striking than Crystal.

"Wow! He will win the judges' hearts when you show him," I declared, stroking his silky coat. Anne was clearly very proud of him, especially as she had bred him.

All the same, I was over the moon with Crystal. I brought her home and introduced her to Tia, Bobby and Jojo.

They gave her a suspicious sniff and then lost interest, indicating that she had been accepted into our little feline family. Crystal seemed unfazed by their indifference and began exploring her new surroundings with curiosity.

When Byron arrived home from school, he was very impressed with the beautiful Chinchilla kitten. However, because of her drunken look, he soon gave Crystal the nickname of 'Boozy'.

Chapter Nine

A New Beginning

I received a phone call from Linda in April. Mark had given up trying to make a go of the pet shop. Instead, he had decided to extend his range of tools, as he had said he would, using the pet shop as an additional shop for his tool hire business.

"I think he made a mistake, not selling animals and birds, because they always help to boost the sale of accessories," Linda reasoned.

"What will you do now?" I asked.

"I shall leave – I don't fancy selling tools as they don't interest me – it sounds boring."

Then Linda made a surprising announcement. "I've decided it's time I became more independent, so I'm going to leave home and get my own place. I've found a small furnished terraced cottage to rent. It's at Dartford, not far from you."

"That's great news!" I exclaimed. "Where in Dartford is it?"

"It's in Little Queen Street."

"I know where that is. It's a narrow cobbled street just off Great Queen Street."

"I've been to see the cottage – it's a really cosy little place. I've signed the papers, and I'll be able to move in next week. I can hardly wait." Linda sounded excited at the prospect of having her own place at last.

"I look forward to visiting you once you've settled in. How will you manage when you're no longer working?"

"I'm searching for another job, but in the meantime, Vick has offered to help with the rent."

I was pleased to hear that Vick was stepping in to help and relieved that Linda had support in this new chapter of her life.

A week later, the posh lady from Sidcup, who wanted to buy my bungalow, arrived to do some measuring. She was still determined to demolish the wall between the lounge and Byron's bedroom to create a large L-shaped lounge. I considered the lounge a good size as it was, extending into a sizeable bay window. Losing a bedroom would probably devalue the property, but it was her decision, so I refrained from commenting.

She stood in the kitchen, planning where to put her white goods. Then she caught sight of the blue pegboard on the wall beside the window and grimaced. "That will definitely have to go," she declared.

When I first saw the grotty pegboard while viewing the bungalow before I bought it, I recall thinking, 'That will definitely have to go.' Seven years later, it was still on the wall, and I no longer paid any mind to it.

The tacky purple nylon carpet in the lounge was a similar story. Left by the previous owners, I had always intended to change it at the first opportunity. But with money tight, something more urgent always took priority, so it remained, showing no sign of wear. I liked the colour purple, but it wasn't a colour I would choose for a carpet. Nevertheless, I ended up buying matching velvet purple curtains.

Now, I planned to take the carpet and curtains to use in the annexe at Rose Cottage, which lacked any furnishings, as I needed to economise as much as possible.

The following week, I received another call from Linda. She had moved into the cottage in Little Queen Street and was keen for me to see her new home so I arranged to visit her the following evening.

Byron and I arrived in the quaint cobbled street and found number eleven. The front door opened from the pavement straight into a small lounge.

Linda greeted us with a beaming smile and hugs. Her younger brother, Jason, was also there, visiting his sister. We exchanged pleasantries, and then Linda gave me a quick tour of the property. The place was impeccably neat, and Linda had managed to infuse it with a homely charm, even placing antimacassars on the armchairs.

From the lounge, narrow stairs led up to a comfortable double bedroom. The compact yet functional kitchen had a bathroom added on at the rear.

"It's a tiny cottage, but it's mine," Linda said with a hint of pride as she put the kettle on for coffee. She was obviously thrilled to have her independence in her very own home.

We settled in the lounge, sipping coffee and catching up for half an hour. Linda told me she had been signed off as sick with a bad back. "The doctor told me that my spine is starting to crumble," she revealed, sounding resigned to what could be a life-changing condition.

"Oh, Linda, that must be so painful for you!" I exclaimed.

Despite the daunting diagnosis, Linda put on a brave front. "It's excruciating at times, but I'm learning to live with it. However, it probably means I won't be able to work again."

"That's so tough, but at least you're entitled to sick pay if you can't work," I told her, trying to emphasise the positive aspects of her situation.

"It's only a pittance, but I can just about manage on it," Linda declared with a smile.

A knock on the front door announced Vick's arrival. He mumbled a brief 'hello' and then whisked Linda upstairs.

Byron and I continued chatting with Jason, trying to ignore the noises coming from the bedroom. They eventually returned downstairs, and I noticed Vick's eyes looked a little bloodshot. I was annoyed that Linda had abandoned us, her guests, to have a romp upstairs with Vick. I concluded that her crumbling spine couldn't be troubling her too much. I decided it was time for Byron and me to return home.

On the 16th of May, the world received worrying news when scientists on the British Antarctic Survey discovered the ozone hole over Antarctica, which helped to put my problems into perspective.

At the beginning of June, Tia began calling again, letting us know in no uncertain terms with her noisy yowls. Bobby Dazzler was starting to mature into a handsome stud cat, but thankfully, he hadn't begun to spray yet.

Although having a maiden queen mated by an inexperienced stud cat wasn't ideal, it was reassuring to see that Bob instinctively knew what to do. Tia seemed keen to be mated by Bob, so I let nature take its course. I was hopeful that, at last, my first litter of Colourpoint kittens was on the way.

Byron and I hadn't seen Joan and Cyril for a long time, so I decided we would pay them a visit at the weekend. I arranged for Roger to care for the cats while we were away.

Summer had arrived, but the weather was unsettled. We drove through heavy rain and reached Thetford on Saturday afternoon.

This was the first time we had seen their supermarket. As we pulled up outside, I was surprised by its ample size.

It was situated in a parade of shops on the edge of a large council estate with a mixture of houses and flats.

The area had a rough edge, so I guessed that Cyril, with his aversion to such environments, wouldn't be very happy living there. He and Joan had both experienced a humble upbringing in a poor area of East London.

They had moved into a council house after their marriage, and Cyril was over the moon when they managed to buy their first house on Fleet Estate in Dartford, leaving their poorer roots behind. They were ecstatic when they ascended the property ladder into a detached executive house in Cox Heath village outside Maidstone. The quality of their lives had improved tremendously.

I realised that returning to live in a rough area, in a flat above a shop, would affect Cyril detrimentally far more than Joan. However, I felt confident in his determination to overcome these challenges, particularly with the promise of the shop's income and the rent from the second flat.

I knew Cyril would enjoy being his own boss and running his own business. This would hopefully compensate for the less-than-ideal urban environment characterised by the constant noise from the street and the lack of green spaces, which were a stark contrast to the peaceful rural village setting he and Joan had been accustomed to.

We entered the shop and found Joan engrossed, working on a checkout till. She spotted us and came over to greet us with a warm hug. She quickly called an assistant to take over at the till and then led us through to a small office at the rear of the shop.

"You seem fairly busy," I remarked. Several customers were browsing in the aisles while others were being served at the deli counter, and a steady queue stood at the two tills.

"Yes, people pop in Saturday afternoon to stock up for the weekend. Cyril has made some improvements to the deli counter. His home-made bread puddings are a big hit with the locals."

"Where is Cyril?" I hadn't noticed him in the shop.

"Oh, he's upstairs, probably watching the CCTV we had installed. He usually vanishes up to the flat during the afternoon to make a start on the dinner. When he's in the shop, he'll only serve on the deli counter or the off-licence."

"It's just as well you've got several assistants to help," I commented.

Joan nodded. "Yes, I couldn't manage without them. Cyril's male ego won't allow him to work on the checkouts or fill the shelves. He thinks it's too demeaning for a manager! I also have to find time to do all the paperwork. There are the accounts and the staff wages to pay. Sunday, when the shop is closed, is the only time I can wash the floor."

I frowned. "So, you're working seven days a week." I was concerned that Joan was taking on far too much work.

"Oh, I'm managing, and the shop is quite a profitable business, which makes it worthwhile. Now, let's go upstairs and see what Cyril is doing. The staff can cope here without me until closing time." She put her arm around Byron's shoulders. "I've missed you - I want to hear all about what you've been up to lately."

We left the shop and walked to the end of the parade. Turning the corner, Joan guided us up a stone stairway to the flats above the shops.

"These flats are actually two-storey maisonettes," Joan said, opening the front door to one of the flats. As we entered, she called out to Cyril.

We found him in the lounge, studying the CCTV footage. He jumped up and hugged us, pleased to see us again.

184

"Dinner is cooking – it should be ready before too long. I'll put the kettle on for some tea."

"This is a lovely, bright room," I remarked, gazing around.

The space was well-utilised, with their furniture and knick-knacks adding a personal touch. At the far end, a large picture window offered a view of the community centre, where some teenagers were hanging around, sheltering from the rain while listening to music on their ghetto blasters. The sound of the newly released 'Power of Love' by Jennifer Rush drifted up to us.

Joan sighed. "It's not very peaceful living here on an estate, but we've learned to adapt and just put up with the noise."

Cyril brought in a tray of drinks from the kitchen, and we sat, catching up with our news while trying to ignore the rowdy noise coming through the window.

Cyril had prepared a tasty shepherd's pie for dinner, followed by a delicious apple tart from the shop. "At least we're never short of food with a supermarket at our disposal," he remarked with a smile, handing me a slice of tart.

"We tend to eat the food that has reached its use-by date. It saves wasting it," Joan said. "It's still perfectly safe to eat," she added, seeing Byron pull a face and pause with a spoonful of tart halfway to his mouth.

The next morning, I anxiously peered through the bedroom curtains to check that my car remained intact. I was worried in case the wheels had been removed during the night. Fortunately, they were all still in place.

After breakfast, Byron and I went down to the shop with Joan to lend a hand. Byron tidied the shelves, and I reorganised the greeting cards while Joan washed the floor.

When we returned to the flat, Cyril had a delicious lunch ready. The aroma of his home-made soup simmering on the stove filled the air, making it a perfect meal to end our visit.

We said goodbye after lunch and thanked Joan and Cyril for having us. "It won't be too long until we are also living in Norfolk," I said as we were leaving.

"It will be wonderful having you all living near us once again," Joan declared excitedly. She gave Byron a hug. "Especially you," she added.

I planned to visit Stella and Mick while we were in Norfolk. Mick was home from Saudi Arabia for a short break, so we could see them both and baby Stewart.

"Give them our love," Cyril called out as they waved goodbye to us.

We arrived in the familiar village of Swanton Morley and parked on the drive of number three Bedingfield Road, a house we knew well. This was where Joan and Cyril started their new life in Norfolk.

It was lovely to see Stella and Mick after such a long time. They were now the proud parents of baby Stewart, a seven-month-old bundle of joy, who I got to cuddle for the first time.

We sat in the lounge, chatting over tea and biscuits. Stella wanted to hear all about the pet shop and Rose Cottage. Mick was eager to see Rose Cottage while he was home, and since the property was empty, he suggested we drive over to Whissonsett, as it wasn't too far. Stella was also keen, so we all piled into my car for the short journey.

As we turned in at the open gate, Stella and Mick were in awe of the expansive grounds.

"This property is absolutely stunning!" Stella exclaimed. "And the annexe looks like a second house."

We climbed out of the car, and Stella rushed over to the sash windows to take a peek inside. Mick followed, carrying Stewart. We couldn't go indoors because we had no keys, so we walked around the cottage, peering in the windows.

As we stared into the lounge, Mick suddenly said, "I'm sure that floor isn't level. It looks as if it's sloping."

I stared hard at the carpeted floor. "It looks fine to me," I concluded, and Stella agreed.

"No, I'm sure I'm right," Mick insisted. "The next time you go inside, put a bowl of water on the lounge floor, and you will see that the floor isn't level."

I promised Mick that I would since he was so adamant.

After thoroughly exploring the front, rear, and side gardens, we drove around the village.

"Look, there's the butcher's just across the road from Rose Cottage, and there's a village store, too," Stella observed as we passed by. "That's really convenient. Most Norfolk villages don't have any shops."

"There's also the post office store on the High Street," I said as I turned down a small side lane.

"Oh, look, there's the village well!" Mick exclaimed, pointing to a round, brick structure with a tiled roof and a small door. A metal handle stuck out on one side. The well was set back from the lane on a patch of grass that led to a turnstile guarding the entrance to a footpath.

I stopped, and we got out to inspect the well. Byron opened the door, and we peered inside. A metal grating covered the top of the well, and the water beneath was crystal clear, showing rocks at the bottom.

"This was where the villagers came for their water before it was piped into the village," Stella said. "It makes an attractive feature – I'm glad it wasn't simply demolished."

We climbed back into the car, and I drove to Swanton Morley to drop off Stella, Mick and Stewart because it was time for Byron and me to return home to Kent.

Now that Linda lived near me, she liked to pop in occasionally for a coffee and a chat.

One morning, as we chatted over coffee in my lounge, she confessed that she still missed her dad dreadfully. I could tell how much her father's passing had affected her.

"I've been toying with the idea of holding a séance to try and contact him. I just want to be sure he's happy in the afterlife, to give me peace of mind," she explained. "I recall you mentioning that you held séances years ago when you lived in London. Would you help me hold a séance, as you know what to do?"

I was surprised and not too keen on Linda's request. The séances I held in London as a teenager had been pretty worrying. There had been murderers coming through with frightening messages. I am older and, I hope, a little wiser these days.

"I'm not sure it's a good idea to delve into the supernatural," I warned her.

Despite my reservations, Linda's determination to hold a séance was unshakable, and she eventually persuaded me to have one. "I'll come round tomorrow afternoon and bring Jason as he's coming to see me. I know he'd be eager to be included if it means we can connect with Dad."

The following afternoon, while Byron was still at school, I set up the coffee table in the lounge as an Ouija board, with letters of the alphabet around the edges and a 'yes' and 'no' card at either end. In the centre, I placed an upturned glass tumbler. I still harboured doubts, but Linda was so keen on holding a séance that I didn't want to disappoint her.

She arrived with Jason, looking excited. They were eager to get started. We sat around the coffee table, each with a finger placed lightly on top of the glass. I told Linda to ask her dad to come through as I felt it was more likely to work if she asked rather than me.

After several minutes of tense anticipation, the glass finally stirred. It began to move hesitantly, then gained a smoother, more confident rhythm as it responded to Linda's questions. The spirit coming through claimed to be her dad. It provided convincing answers that left Linda in no doubt that she was actually communicating with him.

Eventually, the glass came to a halt. Jason was keen to continue, wanting to see who else might come through with messages, but I put my foot down.

"This isn't a game to be trifled with, and I definitely don't want to risk bringing evil spirits into my home."

With the séance over, Linda and Jason were filled with relief and joy. They were confident they had made a genuine connection with their dad. They returned home with buoyant steps, feeling their emotional bond with their father was restored and strengthened.

By the end of June, Tia's nipples had pinked up, confirming that she was pregnant. This prompted me to get the necessary forms from the Governing Council of the Cat Fancy, the regulatory body for cat breeding, to apply for a prefix. This would make the official naming of her kittens much easier, and it was essential if I wanted to become a fully-fledged breeder. I sent off the completed forms with the appropriate fee, asking for my prefix to be registered as Shawpaws. If this name hadn't been used already, it would be allocated to me for my sole use.

At the beginning of July, I received the news I had been waiting for. The solicitor rang to say the contracts had been exchanged on Rose Cottage, and we had a confirmed completion date of Monday, August 5th. Knowing that we would soon be occupying our new home, the relief and sense of accomplishment were overwhelming.

With the purchase secured, I could begin to pack in earnest, sorting out what I wanted to take to Norfolk and what could be discarded.

On Saturday, July 13th, a momentous event took place - the Live Aid pop concert, held in London and Philadelphia simultaneously. I was glued to the television, watching this major spectacle that raised over £50 million for famine relief in Ethiopia.

The concert was opened by Status Quo and featured iconic performances from Queen, U2, David Bowie, and many more. The performances were powerful, and the

189

event was acknowledged worldwide as a fantastic achievement. It had all evolved from an idea by Bob Geldof and Midge Ure, who were much admired for their humanitarian efforts.

I eventually heard back from the Governing Council, confirming that my application for the registered prefix, Shawpaws, had been accepted. I was thrilled to reach this significant milestone in my cat-breeding journey.

Now that Roger and Shelley had been living together for a while, they decided to seal their relationship by taking the next big step and tying the knot. The date of their wedding was set for Saturday, July 27th, at Gravesend registry office, the same venue where Stuart and I were married back in 1970.

As the wedding day approached, I treated myself to a new pale grey suit with matching accessories and a pretty pink blouse. Mum also treated herself to a new pink outfit for this special occasion. I could tell she was a little apprehensive about coping without Dad's support at their son's wedding. It was a bittersweet moment, as we all missed Dad's presence, but we knew he was there with us in spirit, celebrating this special day.

As we all gathered at the registry office on that warm and sunny Saturday morning, Shelley, in her elegant cream dress, couldn't resist complaining about Roger's laid-back attitude.

"It's our wedding day, and while I'm panicking and worrying if I've remembered everything, Roger just lies in bed, calmly reading his car magazine!" she exclaimed, her tone a mixture of exasperation and amusement.

Roger grinned. "I don't know what there was to panic about. We only had to get ready and then drive here."

The ceremony went smoothly, with the registrar's calm and professional demeanour setting a completely different tone from the woman officiating at my wedding. Her ridiculous, theatrical voice had sent us all into convulsions of giggles, turning the solemn occasion into a farce.

The wedding breakfast was held at a nearby pub, followed by the reception in a room appropriately decorated for the occasion. Mum was overjoyed to see her eldest sister, Dora, arrive, accompanied by her son, Lawrence. He had driven his mum to the reception, a lengthy journey from Surrey.

We spent most of the evening catching up with them, sharing our excitement about our upcoming move to Norfolk. Like Mum, having been raised at Ivy House in the depths of rural Suffolk, Auntie Dora and Lawrence were eager to hear all about Rose Cottage.

At the end of the evening, Roger and Shelley left for their two-week honeymoon in the Algarve, so they would miss our moving day, which was a little disappointing. However, they promised to visit us as soon as they returned.

August arrived, and while I'm still busy packing, I'm also keeping a close eye on Tia. Her tummy has expanded as the litter she is carrying grows. So far, she has enjoyed a problem-free pregnancy and is due to give birth any day now. I desperately hoped the litter wouldn't arrive on moving day. I had made her a comfortable bed in a box, and now she was keen to turn it into a nest.

With just two days until the move, Tia gave birth on the 3rd of August to four healthy kittens, one boy and three girls. They were tiny bundles of fur with their eyes tightly shut. The colouring on their points wouldn't develop for a few days, making it difficult to guess what colour they were.

I was concerned about how Tia would cope with the upheaval of the move while nursing a very young litter. I wanted to make the transition as calm and undramatic as possible for her. Ensuring the comfort and well-being of her and her kittens were my top priorities.

Our moving day finally arrived almost one year after we first saw Rose Cottage. It felt like a lifetime had passed since that initial viewing. The day began early, with me bustling about, tackling the last-minute tasks: dismantling the beds with Byron's assistance and packing the bedding and curtains.

Our dear friends and former neighbours, Colin Bullinaire and his mother, played a crucial role in kick-starting our moving day. Their generous offer to collect the keys and prepare the rooms at Rose Cottage for our arrival was a huge relief. Their concern was evident, knowing the property had been vacant for two years, and their thoughtful gesture was much appreciated, especially since we probably wouldn't reach the cottage until late afternoon. Their support made the process feel more manageable.

Colin, a seasoned mover, had given me some valuable tips, including the importance of having a box with everything needed for a cup of tea and a snack when arriving at a new house and keeping that labelled box handy in the car.

The removal firm had calculated that one large van would accommodate all the furniture from both our properties. I hoped they were right and the moving operation would proceed smoothly.

I took special care to ensure the safety and comfort of our four cats. I placed them in secure baskets and kept them in the bathroom, away from the hustle and bustle of the moving process. Tia and her four kittens looked contented in the largest basket. Despite their tender age and fragility, the kittens were thriving.

All our cats, plus Mum and her cherished Thomas, a tabby and white neutered cat, would accompany us in the car.

Mum had acquired Thomas from Stella when he was one year old. Back then, Stella was living with Pete and working full-time. She didn't like leaving Thomas alone in the house all day, so she offered him to Mum, who insisted he must be neutered before she could agree to have him.

Thomas sported distinctive witches' thumbs on his large white front paws, making him look like he was wearing boxing gloves.

With their impressive efficiency, the removal men had my furniture neatly packed in their van by 10 a.m., leaving ample space for Mum's furniture.

Shelley's parents, John and Gwen, had generously offered to take the gardening tools from my shed in their car and hand them over to Roger and Shelley to bring to Rose Cottage once they had returned from their honeymoon.

John and Gwen drew up outside on the green and waited for the removal men to finish loading up. When the removal men were ready to leave, they drove their van out of my driveway and parked on the road so that John could park his car on my drive.

But disaster struck as John attempted to park in the parking area where the caravan had once stood. He misjudged and overshot the edge. One of his front wheels dropped nearly a foot onto the lawn. We stood, looking horrified at the poor car, leaning at an angle, wondering how to rescue it.

John seemed unfazed by the accident. "Well, I don't know how I managed to do that!" he exclaimed with a wry smile. His nonchalance in the face of the car's plight was almost comical, adding a touch of humour to the otherwise tense situation.

"Don't worry about us. You get off to your mum's and leave us to sort this out," Gwen insisted. I felt torn, hating to leave them in such a predicament, but I had no choice. The cats and Byron were in the car, and the removal men were waiting for me to show them the way to Mum's house. I could only hope they would be able to sort out their car without too much trouble.

Just when I thought things couldn't get any more complicated, the new owner from Sidcup arrived, eager to take possession of the keys to her new home. I quickly handed her the keys before climbing into my Escort, anxious to escape. As I reversed out of the drive, she came running after me.

"Have you left your new address in case I need to forward your mail?"

"Er, yes – I left it on the worktop in the kitchen," I lied, knowing that I deliberately hadn't left a forwarding address. I had yet to hear from the VAT man and was worried that I might receive a bill, even though the shop had shown a loss. I hoped he wouldn't be able to trace me once I'd moved.

I finally drove away with a feeling of sadness. It was hard to bid farewell to the cosy bungalow that had been our home for eight years. As we left, I could see poor John and Gwen still struggling to extricate their car.

The removal van followed me on the short journey to Mum's house, a house I had grown up in since the age of eighteen months. As I drove around the Crescent, I spotted Mum strolling along, carrying a shopping bag and looking as if she didn't have a care in the world. I pulled up and called out to her. She came over to the car, looking surprised.

"I was just popping out to the shops to get some rolls for the journey," she told me.

"There isn't time," I yelled. "The removal van is here. You need to return home straight away."

Mum hurried home to unlock the front door while I parked by the green, leaving room for the removal van to pull in behind me.

As the removal men loaded their van with Mum's furniture, she was busy saying her final goodbyes to the neighbours she had known for so many years. She was excited about the move to Norfolk and the prospect of returning to her rural roots, having been born and raised in the adjoining county of Suffolk. However, Mum looked a little sad as she bid farewell to the house she and Dad had called home for over thirty-five years.

The new owners arrived, so Mum handed them the keys before settling into the passenger seat beside me with Thomas in a basket, perched on her lap. Byron sat in the back seat with a cat basket on either side of him. One was Tia's so that he could keep a watchful eye on her and the kittens. The two other baskets were stowed safely in the back of the estate.

We set off filled with anticipation and excitement for our new life in rural Norfolk with the promise of a fresh start. Yet, we felt a touch of nostalgia for the familiar surroundings we were leaving behind.

A removal man had asked me about the property we were moving to. When I explained that it was a cottage in a small Norfolk village, he firmly predicted that we would hate the solitude and be moving back to civilisation in a town before too long. I knew in my heart that he was wrong. After all the stress of the last year, running the pet shop, quiet solitude was exactly what I needed. But I couldn't shake off the worry about Byron. I only hoped that he would be able to adjust to a quieter way of life. Fourteen was not a good age to be uprooted, thrown into a Norfolk village, and expected to attend a new school where he knew no one. His ability to adjust to our new life constantly concerned me.

We stopped for a snack at lunchtime and then continued our journey, realising the removal van would arrive at Rose Cottage before us. At least we didn't need to worry, knowing that Mrs Bullinaire and Colin would be there when the van arrived.

Today, we found ourselves on a different road. I was searching for the turning to Whissonsett, but it eluded me. Fearing I had missed it, I took the next turning, hoping it would lead us to the village. As I drove along the single-track narrow lane with grass growing along the centre, I began to have misgivings. The lane seemed seldom used. However, it eventually led us to the village of Tittleshall, the next village to Whissonsett. I had turned off the main road a little too soon.

We drove through the village until a signpost guided us to Whissonsett. I breathed a sigh of relief as we bowled along another lane on the last leg of our journey with a car full of cats.

Upon our arrival at Rose Cottage, we were greeted by a sight we hadn't anticipated. The gate had been removed and laid on the front lawn so the large removal van could fit through the entrance between the two pillars.

As I parked on the drive, our astonishment grew as we witnessed the removal men hoisting a chest of drawers up to a bedroom window as it wouldn't fit up the stairs. They had even gone to the extent of removing the sash window to prevent any damage to the frame.

Mum leapt out of the car and stood Thomas' basket on the drive, then yelled at the men to stop. "That chest of drawers should be going into the annexe."

The men lowered the chest of drawers back to the ground, muttering to themselves while we went indoors, searching for Mrs Bullinaire and Colin.

We found Mrs Bullinaire on her hands and knees in the lounge, cleaning the fireplace. Colin appeared from the kitchen, beaming and carrying a dustpan and brush. We greeted each other with hugs. Mrs Bullinaire had soot smudged on her face but was in good spirits.

"A neighbour called in at lunchtime with a flask of tea," Colin informed us. "She introduced herself as Mrs Mason, and, to our amusement, she mistook us for the new owners!"

"I think she just wanted an excuse to meet her new neighbours," Mrs Bullinaire remarked.

"You've arrived in time to direct the men where to put the furniture," Colin announced. "When they've finished unloading and gone, I'll treat us all to a fish and chip supper. It'll be your first meal in your new home."

My first priority was to settle the cats in an empty bedroom where they could rest undisturbed. I was relieved that Tia and her kittens seemed unfazed by the upheaval and the long journey. Their resilience reassured me that they would adapt well to their new environment.

My second priority was to find a bowl and fill it with water. I placed it in the middle of the lounge to check that the floor was level. My actions mystified everyone around me except Byron, so I felt an explanation was called for. To my relief, the floor did prove to be level. Evidently, Mick was mistaken when he insisted that the floor sloped.

Now that I was mortgage-free, I was hopeful for more success in my new vocation as a Persian cat breeder than with the disastrous pet shop, where I had learned many hard lessons. I felt optimistic, anticipating a brighter future in our new rural idyll at Rose Cottage.

Appendix

Now that my days in the pet shop were behind me, I found the best way to recall some of the good and bad moments was through the medium of a poem. I have included it here as an additional item of interest.

Nightmare in a Pet Shop

Out in the storeroom, cobwebs hang thickly,
Back in the shop, the bell jangles quickly.
Hope the cat baskets balanced over the door,
Miss the customer and hit the floor.

Pedro screeches from up on his perch,
The canaries shrill out like choirboys in church,
The cockatiels answer from their cage on the shelf;
This pandemonium is bad for my health.

Can't get through the passage for hay and straw,
Bags of sawdust piled up by the door.
Looks like the hay man has left far too much.
Why is that rabbit out of its hutch?

The goldfish swim fast, eluding the net,
Two little boys are making a bet.
The impatient queue is getting irate,
I do wish these fish would cooperate.

The weather is warm, so put Pedro outside
Knowing the passers-by, he'll deride.
Wolf whistles he blasts as the girls saunter by.
They blame the workmen on scaffolds up high.

Rabbits are busy; in the back room, they breed,
Daffy Duck contentedly munches on weed.
The geese being boarded nest in the sinks;
The meat man arrives with green tripe that stinks.

Piles of meat to be weighed, packed and frozen.
Dog discs await engraving by the dozen -
The sound reminds me of a dentist's drill.
This power cut means we can't open the till.

In the morning, I find the cockatiels in flight.
Fluttering freely in the shop through the night.
Grabbing a net, I round up the flock
But manage, in the process, to demolish my stock.

The grass snake, Houdini, escapes through the door;
The chemist opposite spots something on his floor.
He's shocked to discover a snake long and fat,
Curled up, sound asleep on his mat.

Pedro lands with a squawk on a customer's coat;
I reassure her he won't go for her throat.
Unconvinced, she screams and runs for the door;
Alas, another customer I'll see no more.

Don't sell white mice wholesale by the bunch,
They'll only end up as a predator's lunch.
Don't weigh slug pellets in scales used for food
Or the animals' health will no longer be rude.

Weighing wild birdseed and peanuts galore
Means autumn and winter are with us once more.
Taking the orders for sackfuls of coal,
I spy a fat hamster as he goes down a hole.

Puppy pooh beneath the table;
That parrot has chewed up every last label.
Mysterious skid marks in Daffy Duck's mess;
The hamster's abode we can only guess.

The Saturday boy comes to clean out the cages;
He's been out in that back room for simply ages.
His coffee's gone cold; better check he's okay;
Find he's firmly stuck, keeping a deluge at bay.

In fear, he cowers beneath the hutches;
In his arms, an extinguisher he clutches.
He daren't move his thumb, or a flood will occur
And the rabbits will end up with sopping wet fur.

Loosening his grip on the button is hard,
Unlock the back door and dash into the yard.
Aim the extinguisher over the wall,
Then hide when my neighbour begins to bawl.

The soggy shopkeeper comes in to complain,
"By the way, your hamsters drive me insane.
Behind the skirtings, they fight and breed."
He demanded some traps, so I reluctantly agreed.

Behind the chest freezer, a scratching is heard,
So, feet waving wildly and feeling absurd,
Wedged upside down and clutching a net,
I try to capture the recalcitrant pet.

Success as the hamster is caught at last.
I try to get out but find I'm stuck fast.
I'm weary of playing an inverted clown,
If this gets out, I'll be the joke of the town.

Linda tugs me free with a customer's help
But the hamster nips, and she gives a yelp.
In the ensuing confusion, hammy escapes to his lair,
And the terrified customer leaps onto a chair.

Maggots squirm amongst the birdseed.
In its food bowl, a rabbit has peed.
The dustmen are coming – where is the key?
"Linda, please make me a strong cup of tea."

Weed in the sink for cleaning and bunching,
Underfoot, the 'roaches are crunching.
Leeches sucking up the sink sides,
Overhead, the hairy tarantula hides.

Blood and gore splattered inside the cages.
Gerbils, overnight, have fought for ages.
Quick fetch the butcher - he'll know what to do;
Any dead ones must be flushed down the loo.

Feed dead fish to the hungry grass snake -
A tasty snack they surely will make.
Pluck the weevils from the dog meal,
And hope the gerbils' wounds will heal.

A customer wants his dog's temperature taken
But we have no thermometers, if I'm not mistaken.
Linda, mishearing, found one for a tank;
The customer looked horrified, and my heart sank.

The thermometer Linda was cheerfully waving,
Measured six by one inches - had she gone raving?
I explained for a dog, not a tank, it was needed.
Linda, embarrassed; her error conceded.

It's Saturday morning, the shop is busy;
A loud request puts customers in a tizzy.
"Have you got a cure for my dog's wind?"
"Try a cork," I retort, "and don't feed food tinned."

In comes a man sporting a brolly
Demanding to buy a Tortie Trolley
Used during the war on undercover missions,
By tortoises employed by the allied divisions.

I laugh uncontrollably at his tall tale;
"It's true," he insists and gives more detail
Then reveals a mike tucked into his brolly.
It's a joke for the radio - what a wally!

At weekends, Pedro comes home for a break
Where he struts on the table and steals all the cake.
He strips off the wallpaper and frightens the cats;
Laughs at my guests and poops on their hats!

Enough is enough, this shop I must sell;
My health is declining in this living hell.
My disc has slipped from cash and carrying;
I must leave now with no further tarrying.

———————

www.ingramcontent.com/pod-product-compliance
Ingram Content Group UK Ltd.
Pitfield, Milton Keynes, MK11 3LW, UK
UKHW021125240325
456642UK00006B/430

9 781917 601665